Best Easy Day Hikes
Charleston, South Carolina

Help Us Keep This Guide Up to Date

Every effort has been made by the author and editors to make this guide as accurate and useful as possible. However, many things can change after a guide is published—trails are rerouted, regulations change, techniques evolve, facilities come under new management, etc.

We would appreciate hearing from you concerning your experiences with this guide and how you feel it could be improved and kept up to date. While we may not be able to respond to all comments and suggestions, we'll take them to heart, and we'll also make certain to share them with the author. Please send your comments and suggestions to the following address:

FalconGuides
Reader Response/Editorial Department
246 Goose Lane
Guilford, CT 06437

Or you may e-mail us at: editorial@falcon.com

Thanks for your input, and happy trails!

Best Easy Day Hikes Series

Best Easy Day Hikes Charleston, South Carolina

Johnny Molloy

FALCONGUIDES

GUILFORD, CONNECTICUT
HELENA, MONTANA

FALCONGUIDES®

An imprint of Rowman & Littlefield
Falcon and FalconGuides are registered trademarks and Make Adventure Your Story is a trademark of Rowman & Littlefield.
Distributed by NATIONAL BOOK NETWORK

British Library Cataloguing-in-Publication Information available

Library of Congress Cataloging-in-Publication Data

Names: Molloy, Johnny, 1961- author.
Title: Best easy day hikes, Charleston, South Carolina / Johnny Molloy.
Description: Guilford, Connecticut : FalconGuides, [2016] | Series: Best Easy
   Day Hikes Series | "Distributed by NATIONAL BOOK NETWORK"–T.p. verso.
Identifiers: LCCN 2015035857| ISBN 9781493018666 (paperback : alk. paper) |
   ISBN 9781493018673 (e-book)
Subjects: LCSH: Hiking–South Carolina–Charleston Region– Guidebooks. | Trails–South Carolina–Charleston Region–Guidebooks. | Charleston Region (S.C.)–Guidebooks.
Classification: LCC GV199.42.S58 C575 2016 | DDC 917.57/91504– dc23 LC record available at http://lccn.loc.gov/2015035857

♾™ The paper used in this publication meets the minimum requirements of American National Standard for Information Sciences—Permanence of Paper for Printed Library Materials, ANSI/ NISO Z39.48-1992.

Contents

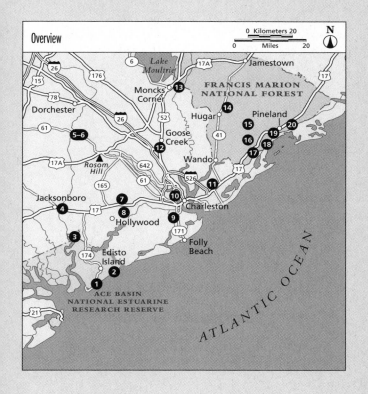

Acknowledgments

Thanks to all the people who helped me with this book, especially David Legere at FalconGuides and my wife Keri Anne. Thanks to DeLorme for their accurate Global Positioning Systems and Sierra Designs for their equipment. Also, thanks to all the park personnel who answered my tireless questions while trying to manage the forests, parks, and preserves of greater Charleston. The biggest thanks go to the local South Carolina hikers and trail builders, as well as those who visit this historic and beautiful slice of America, for without y'all there wouldn't be trails in the first place.

Introduction

The surprising view stretched deep across the marsh toward the Atlantic Ocean. I stood on the wooded bluff. Below me flowed tidal Awendaw Creek. Cape Romain hung low on the horizon. The master path of South Carolina—the Palmetto Trail—had led me to this vista, one of the best easy day hikes in and around Charleston. I mentally reflected on other best easy day hikes included in this guide. Nearby, the Trails of South Tibwin traversed big woods, along ponds and atop open dikes favorable for viewing wildlife and presenting unrivaled views of unbridled nature. The Sewee Shell Ring Interpretive Trail traveled to a 4,000-year-old ceremonial site of aboriginal Lowcountry dwellers. The Ion Swamp Circuit explored brooding, wooded swamps transformed from plantation rice fields. Turkey Creek, a wild creek stream in the Francis Marion National Forest, flowed through deep beech forests sprinkled with wildflowers. Another section of the Palmetto Trail visited mysterious Carolina bay wetlands. Still other trails wound through amenity-heavy county parks, including James Island, Palmetto Islands, and Wannamaker. At these parks, a blend of natural-surface and asphalt paths took me to isolated islands, along estuaries and ponds, as well as by picnic areas, playgrounds, dog parks, and more. Up by Moncks Corner, Old Santee Canal Park harbored a wealth of trails and history set in a scenic preserve, with the add-on of a first-rate, informative visitor center. Of course, Charles Towne Landing, the site of Charleston's first European settlement, remains an unparalleled trail-rich historic destination.

In addition, what would Charleston and the Lowcountry be without oceanic hiking? Botany Bay Wildlife Management Area contained a trail leading to over 2 miles of wild

Atlantic beachfront, enhanced by historical sites within its bounds. The Spanish Mount Trail at Edisto Beach State Park led through coastal maritime woods to an ancient shell midden along salty Scott Creek. Charleston's plantation history was represented—among other places—at ACE Basin National Wildlife Refuge and Dungannon Plantation Heritage Preserve. Both locales are antebellum farms formerly growing rice but converted to wildlife preserves. Nature-oriented Caw Caw Interpretive Center also presented a multiplicity of habitats favorable for wildlife, enhanced by an excellent trail system, guaranteed to keep you coming back time and again. Farther inland, the hikes at Givhans Ferry State Park traversed bluffs harboring both rare plants and a fascinating past from Revolutionary War and Civil War days, as well as deep wild woods. The Edisto Nature Trail used boardwalks to visit ancient oaks, travel colonial roads, and view industrial history, now covered in a veil of incredible bottomland forest.

The splash of nearby kayakers on Awendaw Creek brought me back to the here and now. And yes, not only can you hike this region, but kayak, canoe, camp, swim, and fish. This area is truly a treasure for locals and visitors coming to see this special slice of South Carolina.

With this book in hand and willing feet, you can explore greater Charleston. No matter where you go, the trails in this book will enhance your outdoor experience and leave you appreciating the natural splendors of the Lowcountry. Enjoy.

The Nature of Charleston and the Lowcountry

Charleston and the Lowcountry's hiking grounds range from singletrack wooded trails along creeks and underneath resplendent forest to well-marked nature trails to strolls on asphalt interpretive paths. Hikes in this guide cover the gamut. While by definition a best easy day hike is not strenuous and generally poses little danger to the traveler, knowing a few details about the nature of Charleston and the Lowcountry will enhance your explorations.

Weather

Charleston, South Carolina, experiences all four seasons. Summer is hot and humid, with sporadic sweltering spells and heavy thunderstorms. Dawn hikers can avoid some heat, but summer is the least favorable hiking time. Hiking increases when the first northerly fronts of fall sweep cool clear air across the Lowcountry. Crisp mornings give way to warm afternoons. Fall is drier than summer. Winter will bring occasional frigid days, but most days are fine for hiking. Winter rains will keep you indoors more than will low temperatures. Spring will be more variable. A warm day can be followed by a cold wet one. But any avid hiker will find more good hiking days than they will have time to hike in spring, fall, and winter.

Critters

Charleston trail treaders will encounter mostly benign creatures on these trails, such as deer, squirrels, wild turkeys, a variety of songbirds, and rabbits, but especially deer. Don't be surprised to encounter a black bear in the Francis Marion National Forest. If you do, simply stand back and let it go its way. Avoid direct eye contact. Most likely the bear will quickly scatter from your presence. Never feed a bear under any circumstances. A fed bear is a dead bear. They become food habituated and will do anything to get more of the elixir known as human food. They ultimately are hit by a vehicle, shot, or euthanized. More rarely seen (during the daylight hours especially) are coyotes, raccoons, and opossums. Deer in some of the parks are remarkably tame and may linger on or close to the trail as you approach. If you feel uncomfortable when encountering any critter, keep your distance and they will generally keep theirs.

Be Prepared

Hiking in the greater Charleston area is generally safe. Still, hikers should be prepared, whether they are out for a short stroll at Charles Towne Landing or venturing into secluded sections of the Francis Marion National Forest. Some specific advice:

- Know the basics of first aid, including how to treat bleeding, bites and stings, and fractures, strains, or sprains. Pack a first-aid kit on each excursion.

- Familiarize yourself with the symptoms of heat exhaustion and heat stroke. Heat exhaustion symptoms include heavy sweating, muscle cramps, headache, dizziness, and fainting. Should you or any of your hiking party exhibit any of these symptoms, cool the victim down immediately by rehydrating and getting him or her to an air-conditioned location. Cold showers also help reduce body temperature. Heat stroke is much more serious: The victim may lose consciousness and the skin is hot and dry to the touch. In this event, call 911 immediately.

- Regardless of the weather, your body needs a lot of water while hiking. A full 32-ounce bottle is the minimum for these short hikes, but more is always better. Bring a full water bottle, whether water is available along the trail or not.

- Don't drink from streams, rivers, creeks, or lakes without treating or filtering the water first. Waterways and water bodies may host a variety of contaminants, including giardia, which can cause serious intestinal unrest.

- Prepare for extremes of both heat and cold by dressing in layers.

- Carry a backpack in which you can store extra clothing, ample drinking water and food, and whatever goodies, like guidebooks, cameras, and binoculars, you might want. Consider bringing a GPS with tracking capabilities.

- Cell phone coverage is widespread, but you can never be absolutely sure until you are on location. Bring your device, but make sure you've turned it off or put it on the vibrate setting while hiking. Nothing like a "wake the dead"-loud ring to startle every creature, including fellow hikers.

- Keep children under careful watch. Trails travel along lakes, creeks, tidal streams, and the Atlantic Ocean, some of which are not recommended for swimming. Be watchful around wooded swamps with their cypress knees there to trip the unwary hiker. Hazards along some of the trails include poison ivy, uneven footing, and tidal muck; make sure children don't stray from the designated route. Children should carry a plastic whistle; if they become lost, they should stay in one place and blow the whistle to summon help.

Zero Impact

Trails in the greater Charleston area are well used year-round. We as trail users must be especially vigilant to make sure our passage leaves no lasting mark. Here are some basic guidelines for preserving trails in the region:

1. Pack out all your own trash, including biodegradable items like orange peels. You might also pack out garbage left by less considerate hikers.

2. Don't approach or feed any wild creatures—the ground squirrel eyeing your snack food is best able to survive if it remains self-reliant.

3. Don't pick wildflowers or gather rocks, shells, feathers, and other treasures along the trail, especially aboriginal and settler relics. Removing these items will only take away from the next hiker's experience and steal a piece of the historic puzzle that is Charleston's past.

4. Avoid damaging trailside soils and plants by remaining on the established route. This is also a good rule of thumb for avoiding poison ivy and other common regional trailside irritants.

5. Be courteous by not making loud noises while hiking.

6. Many of these trails are multiuse, which means you'll share them with other hikers, trail runners, mountain bikers, and equestrians. Familiarize yourself with the proper trail etiquette, yielding the trail when appropriate.

7. Use outhouses at trailheads or along the trail.

Charleston Area Boundaries and Corridors

For the purposes of this guide, best easy day hikes are confined to a 1-hour drive from Charleston, South Carolina.

Two major interstates and a major highway stretch out from Charleston. Directions to trailheads are given from these interstates and arteries. They are I-26, I-526, and US 17.

Land Management

The following government organizations manage most of the public lands described in this guide, and can provide further information on these hikes and other trails in their service areas.

Francis Marion National Forest, 2967 Steed Creek Rd., Huger, SC 29450, (843) 336-3248, www.fs.usda .gov/main/scnfs/

South Carolina Department of Parks, Recreation and Tourism, 205 Pendleton St., Columbia, SC 29201, (803) 734-0156, southcarolinaparks.com

Charleston County Park & Program Services, 861 Riverland Dr., Charleston, SC 29412, (843) 795-4386, ccprc.com/

How to Use This Guide

This guide is designed to be simple and easy to use. Each hike is described with a map and summary information that delivers the trail's vital statistics including length, difficulty, fees and permits, park hours, canine compatibility, and trail contacts. Directions to the trailhead are also provided, along with a general description of what you will see along the way. A detailed route finder (Miles and Directions) sets forth mileages between significant landmarks along the trail.

Hike Selection

This guide describes trails that are accessible to every hiker, whether visiting from out of town or someone lucky enough to live in the Charleston area. The hikes are no longer than 5.4 miles round-trip, and most are considerably shorter. They range in difficulty from flat excursions perfect for a family outing to more challenging treks. While these trails are among the best, keep in mind that nearby trails, often in the same park or preserve, may offer options better suited to your needs. I've sought to space hikes throughout the greater Lowcountry region, so wherever your starting point, you'll find a great easy day hike nearby.

Difficulty Ratings

These are all easy hikes, but easy is a relative term. To aid in the selection of a hike that suits particular needs and abilities, each is rated easy, moderate, or more challenging. Bear in mind that even most challenging routes can be made easy by hiking within your limits and taking rests when you need them.

Easy hikes are generally short and flat, taking no longer than an hour to complete.

Moderate hikes involve increased distance and relatively mild changes in elevation and will take 1 to 2 hours to complete.

More challenging hikes feature some steep stretches, greater distances, and generally take longer than 2 hours to complete.

These are completely subjective ratings—consider that what you think is easy is entirely dependent on your level of fitness and the adequacy of your gear (primarily shoes). If you are hiking with a group, you should select a hike with a rating that's appropriate for the least fit and prepared in your party.

Approximate hiking times are based on the assumption that on flat ground, most walkers average 2 miles per hour. Adjust that rate by the steepness of the terrain (of which there isn't much in the Lowcountry) and your level of fitness (subtract time if you're an aerobic animal and add time if you're hiking with kids), and you have a ballpark hiking duration. Be sure to add more time if you plan to picnic or take part in other activities like bird watching or photography.

Trail Finder

Best Hikes for River and Lake Lovers

Best Hikes for Children

Best Hikes for Dogs

Best Hikes for Saltwater Lovers

Best Hikes for Solitude

Best Hikes for History Buffs

Best Hikes for Nature Lovers

Map Legend

Symbol	Description	Symbol	Description
══26══	Interstate Highway	‿	Bridge
══52══	US Highway	▲	Campground
══41══	State Highway	▲	Campsite
══FR243══	Forest/County Road	—	Dam
━━━━━	Local Road	⌶	Gate
= = = = =	Unimproved Road	▲	Mountain/Hill
▬▬▬▬▬	Featured Trail	🅿	Parking
- - - - -	Trail	🌲	Picnic Area
‖‖‖‖‖‖‖	Boardwalk	■	Point of Interest/Structure
～～～	River/Creek	🏠	Ranger Station
—·—·—	Intermittent Stream	🚻	Restrooms
- · - · -	Marsh/Swamp	o⌐	Spring
⬭	Body of Water	⌸	Tower
▲	National Forest/Park	o	Town
▲	Local/State Park	8	Trailhead
═	Bench	⬱	Viewpoint/Overlook
➤	Boat Launch	❓	Visitor/Information Center

1 Edisto Beach State Park Hike

The hike travels to an ancient shell mound known as the Spanish Mount, situated on the banks of tidal Scott Creek. First, leave one of the state park campgrounds, then wander through maritime hardwoods, coming along Scott Creek, where marsh views await. Continue under live oaks, cedars, and palms to the stabilized shell midden, where you can see layers of shells piled over time and good panoramas of the surrounding estuary. The Forest Loop adds new trail on your return.

Distance: 3.7-mile balloon loop
Hiking time: 2 to 2.5 hours
Difficulty: Moderate
Trail surface: Natural surface
Best season: Fall through spring
Other trail users: Bicyclers
Canine compatibility: Leashed dogs permitted
Fees and permits: Entrance fee required

Schedule: 8 a.m.–6 p.m. daily (extended during Daylight Savings Time)
Maps: Edisto Beach State Park Trails; USGS Edisto Island, Edisto Beach
Trail contacts: Edisto Beach State Park, 8377 State Cabin Rd., Edisto Island, SC 29438, (843) 869-2156, southcarolina parks.com

Finding the trailhead: From exit 212B on I-526 west near Charleston (the end of I-526 West), take Sam Rittenburg Boulevard a short distance to US 17. Turn right on US 17 south and follow it for 19.1 miles to SC 174. Turn left (south) on SC 174 and follow it 20.8 miles to the right turn onto State Cabin Road, before you reach the main beach entrance on your left. Follow State Cabin Road 0.5 mile to the parking area on your right, near the Live Oak campground. GPS trailhead coordinates: N32° 30.702', W80° 18.156'

The Hike

A trip to Edisto Beach State Park is a trip to yesteryear. This quaint park lies next to a small vacation village, with no high rises and very few chain stores. Edisto Beach has been dubbed "Mayberry by the Sea." Edisto Beach, 20 miles off South Carolina's main coastal drag, US 17, is at the end of a dead-end road. Despite the location, this park and community are a place of return. Families who come here to visit come here year after year and bring their kids, who in turn bring their kids.

You will find the hiking trails here an added bonus. Our hike leads to the Spanish Mount, an ancient Indian midden. This shell mound, built up in a circle and filled in the middle, though known as the Spanish Mount, has nothing to do with Spaniards. The midden, mostly of shells, dates back around 4,000 years. Mounds of shells at rich estuarine areas are not uncommon in the Southeast, but the ringed shape of this mound and name Spanish Mount remain a mystery, though the circular nature of the midden lends credence to it being a ceremonial site. The Spanish Mount is, however, purportedly the second oldest pottery site in South Carolina. Deer, rabbit, turkey, and bones of fourteen types of fish have been found here, as well as potshards. A viewing platform has been installed where you can look out on Scott Creek below and into a cut in the mound, showing layer upon layer of shells. This platform also serves to check the erosion of the site as has happened over time by the ceaseless tides of Scott Creek. In 1809, it was reported to be 20 feet high and a half-acre in size. Today, it is one-tenth that size . . .

This hike starts near the Live Oak camping area. Edisto Beach State Park has two camping areas offering different atmospheres. The main camping area is the most popular and is just a dune away from the Atlantic Ocean with a creek on the mainland side of the campground. The Live Oak camping area is less popular, simply because it is farther from the beach, and you must drive to the ocean. The main camping area will fill anytime during the summer and reservations are highly recommended from June through August. The campgrounds also see an upsurge in business during spring break, but since alcohol is not allowed a family atmosphere reigns then and throughout the year.

The Spanish Mount Trail leaves the trailhead into a tall shady forest of live oak and loblolly pine with a dense understory of yaupon. Magnolia, cedar, and palm add biodiversity to the trek. The doubletrack path makes for easy hiking. Handy maps are posted at all trail intersections. Pass both ends of the Forest Loop, your return route, then meet the Scott Creek Trail. It heads for the main part of the park but our hike keeps west, coming along the edge of Scott Creek marsh. Enjoy walking in woods and scoping onto the Scott Creek estuary. The maritime woods are a joy through which to travel.

You are almost to the Spanish Mount after meeting the Big Bay Trail, which leads to an alternate trailhead. Soon emerge at a bluff above Scott Creek. Views open in the far and steps lead down to the front of the Spanish Mount in the near. There, you can see the layers of shells deposited over time by aboriginal South Carolinians. The shell midden has been stabilized by the wooden structure along the shore of Scott Creek. Soak in the interpretive information then backtrack toward the trailhead, walking the Forest Loop for variety.

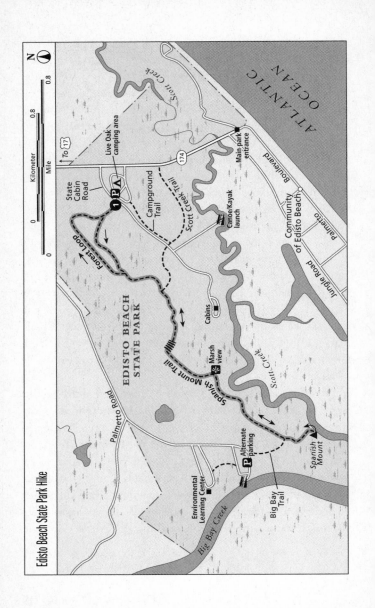

Edisto Beach State Park Hike

ATLANTIC OCEAN

Scott Creek

To 17

Live Oak camping area

State Cabin Road

Forest Loop

Campground Trail

Scott Creek Trail

Main park entrance

Canoe/Kayak launch

Community of Edisto Beach

Palmetto Road

EDISTO BEACH STATE PARK

Cabins

Marsh view

Spanish Mount Trail

Scott Creek

Jungle Road

Palmetto Road

Environmental Learning Center

Alternate parking

Big Bay Trail

Big Bay Creek

Spanish Mount

Kilometer

Mile

0   0.8

N

174

Miles and Directions

0.0 Leave the parking area off Cabin Road and head north on a doubletrack path, the Spanish Mount Trail, in rich woods.

0.1 Stay left on the Spanish Mount Trail as the Forest Loop leaves right.

0.4 Pass the other end of the Forest Loop.

0.6 Keep straight on the Spanish Mount Trail as the Scott Creek Trail heads left.

0.9 Cross a boardwalk over a marshy creek.

1.2 A short track leads left to a view of the Scott Creek marsh.

1.7 The Big Bay Trail leaves right.

1.8 Reach the Spanish Mount. Enjoy the views and interpretive information. Backtrack.

3.2 Head left on the Forest Loop.

3.6 Rejoin the Spanish Mount Trail.

3.7 Return to the trailhead, completing the hike.

2 Botany Bay Beach Walk

Botany Bay Wildlife Management Area is one of South
Carolina's finest coastal treasures, with a large swath of rich
maritime woods, marshy creeks, and 2 miles of wild beaches
to explore. A trail leads from the mainland across a marsh to
the edge of the Atlantic, where one direction takes you to
and through "the Boneyard," where skeletal trees meld with
the shore in a photographer's haven, while the other direction leads to more typical open beachfront toward Townsend
Creek.

Distance: 1 mile there-and-back
Hiking time: 1 to 3 hours
Difficulty: Easy to moderate
Trail surface: Natural surface
Best season: Year-round
Other trail users: None
Canine compatibility: Leashed
dogs permitted
Fees and permits: None

Schedule: Sunrise–30 minutes
after sunset
Maps: Botany Bay WMA; USGS
Rockville
Trail contacts: Botany Bay Plantation Wildlife Management Area,
10666 Botany Bay Rd., Edisto
Island, SC 29438, (843) 869-
2713, dnr.sc.gov/

Finding the trailhead: From exit 212B on I-526 west near
Charleston (the end of I-526 West), take Sam Rittenburg Boulevard
a short distance to US 17. Turn right on US 17 south and follow it
for 19.1 miles to SC 174. Turn left (south) on SC 174 and follow it
17.7 miles to the left turn onto Botany Bay Road. Follow Botany Bay
Road 1.6 miles to the left turn into the WMA. Register just beyond the
gate and continue straight for 1.7 miles to the signed right turn for
the beach. Follow the unnamed road to the beach a short distance
to dead-end at a parking area. GPS trailhead coordinates: N32°
32.960', W80° 14.007'

The Hike

Botany Bay Plantation is a fascinating place, chock full of human and natural history. The site of two pre–Civil War plantations, one of which grew the long and fine Sea Island cotton, Botany Bay contains multiple sites listed on the National Register of Historic Places, including an old plantation site as well as a shell midden thousands of years old. The two plantations, Bleak Hall and Sea Cloud, were later bought and put together as one by a man named Jason Meyer, who established Botany Bay Plantation in the 1930s. He willed the property to the state of South Carolina upon his wife's death. She passed away in 2007 and the Department of Natural Resources opened Botany Bay to the public in 2008. Today, visitors can drive the live oak–shaded lanes and enjoy a 6.5-mile auto tour that visits over a dozen significant sites along the way.

Make sure to add the auto tour to your hike. Along the way you can see the residence of the Meyers, still in use as the DNR property manager's residence. Next, visit the grounds of the Bleak Hall Plantation. Though the main house was burned after the Civil War, you can still see two remaining buildings from the 1800s—the icehouse and gardener hut. Interestingly, the remains of a slave cabin chimney stand as well. Next, pass a barn that was used during World War II to store hay for the US Coast Guard, who patrolled the shores of Edisto Island on horseback, looking for offshore German boats. Ahead, pass fields and other lands managed for wildlife that once grew the Sea Island cotton sought to knit the finest lace by European weavers.

Stop by and see Picnic Pond, and Jason's Lake. Both bodies of water are rich in wildlife from wood ducks to alligators to fish and shorebirds, as well as osprey and eagles. You are now on the property of the other plantation known as Sea Cloud. This plantation had its origin as Revolutionary War land grants. The main plantation building, bordered by elaborate gardens, stood three stories high, with a ballroom occupying the entire third floor. All that remain are brick ruins. Beyond Jason's Lake, a beehive-shaped well from the 1820s can be seen from the auto tour.

By this point, you are probably excited to take the trail to the beach, where natural preserved coastal beauty awaits. The park features 2 miles of pristine beachfront. It is a completely different experience exploring a pure natural ocean environment without having cottages and high-rises stretching behind you. However, before reaching the beach, enjoy the trail leading out to it. You will first follow an elevated roadbed across a tidal, cordgrass marsh. Then you join a hammock island, one of 3,500 of these South Carolina islands located landward of the barrier islands facing the Atlantic, and seaward of the mainland. These relatively undisturbed islands provide isolated habitats for flora and fauna such as the painted bunting, which nests on these hammock islands during the spring and summer. After passing through the small hammock island, the elevated track heads for the Atlantic. Emerge at the ocean. To complete the hike, turn around and follow the path back to the trailhead.

Option: You can simply relax at the end of the trail. Or make your way northeast to the Boneyard, where skeletal trees are embedded into the sandy shoreline, where photographers will be found trying to take the ultimate shot. Or you could head southwest toward Townsend Creek, where the sandy strip widens and becomes more open and typical of South Carolina beaches—sans civilization of course. Try

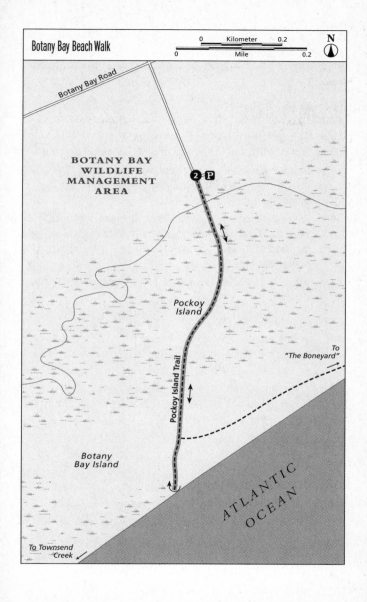

Botany Bay Beach Walk

0   Kilometer   0.2

0   Mile   0.2

N

Botany Bay Road

BOTANY BAY
WILDLIFE
MANAGEMENT
AREA

2 P

Pockoy
Island

Pockoy Island Trail

To
"The Boneyard"

Botany
Bay Island

ATLANTIC
OCEAN

To Townsend
Creek

to time your visit with low tide—it is easier to get around, especially when heading toward the Boneyard. Be apprised there is no shelling allowed and a stiff fine awaits those who break the law.

Miles and Directions

0.0 Pass around the pole gate heading south on the Pockoy Island Trail toward the beach. Enjoy wide views of the marsh.

0.3 Reach Pockoy Island, an isolated hammock island. Pass through the small wooded isle then emerge south, cruising through marsh.

0.5 Reach the beach and Atlantic Ocean after passing through more forest. (**Option:** Now, you can walk left or right along the beach, extending your seaside trek by 4 miles if going to both ends of the beach and back.)

1.0 Retracing your steps, arrive back at the trailhead, completing the hike.

3 ACE Basin Hike

This hike makes a loop in the varied habitats of ACE Basin National Wildlife Refuge. The circuit hike traces an old railroad grade before curving around Goose Pond and other wetlands ideal for waterfowl. It then circles around scenic Alexander Pond, in the shadow of Grove Plantation, an 1828 home that now serves as refuge headquarters. After viewing Grove Plantation loop north back to the trailhead.

Distance: 2.8-mile loop
Hiking time: 1.5 to 2 hours
Difficulty: Easy
Trail surface: Natural surface
Best season: Fall through spring
Other trail users: Bicyclers
Canine compatibility: Leashed dogs permitted
Fees and permits: None

Schedule: Sunrise–sunset
Maps: ACE Basin National Wildlife Refuge–The Grove Plantation; USGS Fenwick
Trail contacts: Ernest F. Hollings ACE Basin National Wildlife Refuge, 8675 Willtown Rd., Hollywood, SC 29449, (843) 889-3084, fws.gov/refuge/ACE_Basin

Finding the trailhead: From exit 212B on I-526 west near Charleston (the end of I-526 West), take Sam Rittenburg Boulevard a short distance to US 17. Turn right on US 17 south and follow it for 19.1 miles to SC 174. Turn left (south) on SC 174 and follow it 3.6 miles to the right turn onto Willtown Road. Follow Willtown Road for 2 miles then turn left onto Jehossee Island Road and follow it 2 miles to the entrance gate of the refuge. Park here. *Note:* The refuge is strictly gated before 8:30 a.m. and after 4 p.m. Monday through Friday, and is closed all weekend so parking outside the entrance gate is encouraged. GPS trailhead coordinates: N32° 40.294', W80° 23.592'

The Hike

Ernest F. Hollings National Wildlife Refuge comprises but 12,000 acres of the greater 1.1-million-acre ACE Basin. This massive estuary is comprised of the lower parts of three rivers—the Ashepoo, Combahee, and Edisto. The basin lands are held by not only the US Fish and Wildlife Service, but also state parks and wildlife management areas. However, they are mostly held in private hands in the form of huge plantations established early in South Carolina's day. Even this wildlife refuge was a former plantation until 1992. The plantation was established back in 1694, as an English land grant to a man named Robert Fenwick. It passed through several owners until George Washington Morris purchased the property in 1825, giving it the name we know today— Grove Plantation.

In 1828, Mr. Morris built the plantation house currently on the grounds. Unfortunately, Mr. Morris only enjoyed his house for 6 years before passing away. His wife, Maria, managed the property until her son took over. Rice was the main agricultural crop and the adjacent swamps were converted to rice fields.

During the Civil War, Grove Plantation was occupied by Confederate soldiers. However, unlike most other area plantations, it was spared a burning. After the war, the land went through more owners, morphing from agricultural use to winter residence and hunting retreat. The land management followed suit, with the former rice fields converted to waterfowl habitats. Eventually, as the ACE Basin project began to take shape, The Nature Conservancy stepped in and purchased Grove Plantation and its property. The next owners were you and I, under the management of the US Fish

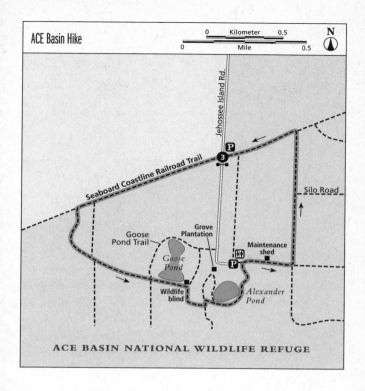

ACE Basin Hike

Kilometer

Mile

N

Jehossee Island Rd.

Seaboard Coastline Railroad Trail

P

3

Silo Road

Goose
Pond Trail

Grove
Plantation

*Goose
Pond*

Maintenance
shed

P

Wildlife
blind

*Alexander
Pond*

ACE BASIN NATIONAL WILDLIFE REFUGE

and Wildlife Service. The Grove Plantation house is deservedly on the National Register of Historic Places.

The ACE Basin is the largest remaining undeveloped estuary on the East Coast of the United States. Habitats range from beaches to barrier islands to tidal marshes to freshwater marshes, creeks, and rivers of all sizes. Since taking over the refuge, the Fish and Wildlife Service has repaired the dikes and gates to manage the wetlands for wildlife as well as sow fields and establish roads and accesses for visitors from hunters to photographers to hikers like us. We first follow the Seaboard Coastline Railroad Trail, a former railroad line under rich woods where birdsong has replaced the whine of rolling steel wheels. The route curves through mixed lands then reaches the Goose Pond, a popular birding destination. Nearby, a large managed impoundment houses water-oriented wildlife from alligators to wood storks. The hike next circles around pretty Alexander Pond then comes to Grove Plantation. Make sure to take time to circle around the building and admire the historic structure and head inside the visitor center if it is open. From there, you head east, passing the maintenance area to pick up a northbound track that returns you to the Seaboard Coastline Railroad Trail. A short walk on the railroad grade returns you to the trailhead.

Miles and Directions

0.0 Leave the parking area by the entrance gate, heading southwest on the Seaboard Coastline Railroad Trail, a former railroad grade.

0.5 Pass a sometimes wet, grass track heading left.

0.6 Leave the railroad grade left as another trail jogs right then continues southwest. Turn south, passing under a small transmission line.

0.8 The trail curves east.

0.9 Cross Dike leaves right, just after a grassy track enters left. Keep straight.

1.2 Reach a four-way intersection. Keep straight as the Goose Pond Trail leaves left. Cross a dike overlooking wetlands on both sides.

1.3 Reach another intersection. Here, the Goose Pond Trail enters left, with an observation deck nearby. Head right, south, curving on a dike to turn easterly.

1.4 Reach a three-way intersection. Head left crossing a bridge over a canal. Immediately head right, east again, toward Alexander Pond. Continue circling around Alexander Pond. Grove Plantation is visible.

1.8 Come near the Grove Plantation parking area and restroom to your left. Feel free to visit the grounds of the historic building, then leave east.

1.9 Pass the refuge maintenance shed on your left, then reach a four-way intersection. Head left, northbound on a grassy track running parallel to a transmission line.

2.3 Keep straight, still northbound, as Silo Road heads east.

2.5 Turn left, back on the Seaboard Coastline Railroad Trail.

2.8 Return to the trailhead, completing the hike.

4 Edisto Nature Trail

This hike may have more highlights per foot than any other trail in this guide. This national recreation trail just off the Edisto River mixes human and natural history as you traverse the Old Charleston Road, the Kings Highway, and a former railroad bed through incredibly lush rich bottomland forest. Visit the site of old Jacksonboro, a rice dike, and an old phosphate mine and plant, barely discernable these days. Natural highlights include a long boardwalk over swamp wetland to a braid of the Edisto River, huge live oaks, wildflowers, and a plethora of everywhere–you–look beauty.

Distance: 1.4-mile loop
Hiking time: 1 to 1.5 hours
Difficulty: Easy, boardwalks can be slippery when wet
Trail surface: Natural surface, lots of boardwalks and bridges
Best season: Year-round
Other trail users: None
Canine compatibility: Leashed dogs permitted

Fees and permits: None
Schedule: Sunrise–sunset
Maps: Edisto Nature Trail; USGS Jacksonboro
Trail contacts: MeadWestvaco, Forestry Division, P.O. Box 118005, Charleston, SC 29423, (843) 871-5000, www.mwv.com

Finding the trailhead: From exit 212B on I-526 west near Charleston (the end of I-526 West), take Sam Rittenburg Boulevard a short distance to US 17. Turn right on US 17 south and follow it for 25.4 miles to the bridge over the Edisto River. The trailhead is on the west side of the Edisto River just after the bridge. GPS trailhead coordinates: N32° 46.142', W80° 27.139'

The Hike

Back in 1968, the National Trail System Act began a system of designating national recreation trails, national scenic trails, and national historic trails. National recreation trails are designated by the secretary of the interior or the secretary of agriculture, recognizing exemplary trails of local and regional significance in response to an application from the trail's managing agency or organization. Through designation, these trails are recognized as part of America's national system of trails.

Westvaco built the Edisto Nature Trail, and it has been under national recreation trail designation since 1976. South Carolina has only seventeen national recreation trails, so having the designation is a big deal. To find out for yourself if the Edisto Nature Trail is deserving of its status, enter the woods, immediately joining the Old Charleston Road, the former track that was replaced by nearby US 17. Imagine early South Carolinians traveling this road. After following the Old Charleston Road a short distance underneath tall pines, you will turn away from it and join yet an older road, the Kings Highway. This route was built by the English between 1650 and 1730, linking the former colonies. At one time, it was the primary land artery across South Carolina. Now, it too is but a faint track in the woods that would be otherwise unidentifiable if not signed. Never in a contiguously good condition, the Kings Highway did connect South Carolina to Boston. However, it was mostly used for postal and short-distance transportation, since moving about by water on the Atlantic was much easier in that day than traveling overland. In 1782, when the British had Charleston under their control, the South Carolina General Assembly met here on the banks of the Edisto. Jacksonboro had become a settlement in the 1730s. The town is now just west of here, on higher ground.

Ahead, the Short Trail leaves left and splits the loop in half, and you leave the Kings Highway. Next, a long boardwalk leads to part of the Edisto River. Along the boardwalk you pass over a scenic and brooding swamp forest. Look for wading birds in the swamp. After returning to the loop, pass the site of a sawmill, ironically set in thick woods. The loop continues and you near a depression covered in saw palmetto that was once the site of an old phosphate mine. Not only are these historic sites interesting, but they also demonstrate the amazing recuperative powers of nature, because they look like perfectly natural woods. And if we needed any more evidence, join a dike that once was part of a rice field. But now you look over nothing but cypress and gum trees, along with maple.

Long boardwalks and bridges continue. Pass a barge canal that once linked to the Edisto River, sending rice to market. Ahead, on high ground, formerly stood a phosphate factory, now woods. Join an old railroad bed that makes for a level track. Finally, the path passes beside some huge live oaks before returning to the trailhead, completing a history-laden hike.

Miles and Directions

0.0 Leave the parking area on US 17. Head southeast, first on the Old Charleston Road, then through woods and onto the Kings Highway, both historic roads now encompassed in bottomland hardwoods. Much of the trail is boardwalks and bridges overlaying woods.

0.2 The Short Trail leads left, cutting across the loop. Stay straight on the main loop.

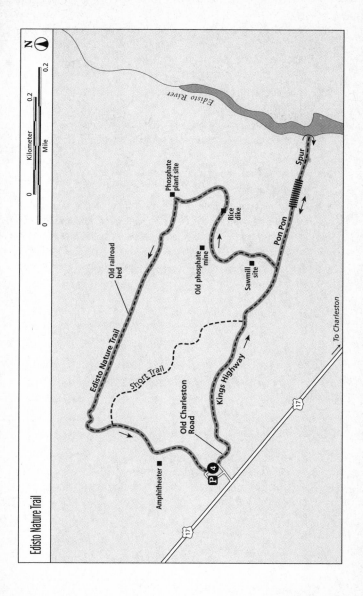

Edisto Nature Trail

N

Kilometer
0   0.2

Mile
0   0.2

Edisto River

Old railroad bed

Phosphate plant site

Edisto Nature Trail

Rice dike

Old phosphate mine

Pon Pon

Spur

Sawmill site

Short Trail

Kings Highway

Old Charleston Road

P 4

Amphitheater

17

17

To Charleston

0.3 Stay straight at the Pon Pon Spur. It soon becomes a long boardwalk over a hardwood swamp. Look for a huge loblolly pine beside the trail. At one point, the boardwalk splits around a large cypress tree.

0.5 Look out on a braid of the Edisto River at boardwalk's end. Backtrack.

0.7 Return to the primary loop, heading right, continuing the counterclockwise loop. Pass a sawmill site, then a phosphate mine and rice dike in succession.

0.9 Turn left at the site of a phosphate factory, soon joining an old logging railroad tram. The way is straight.

1.2 Leave left from the logging tram. Look for huge live oaks and spruce pines. Ahead, the Short Trail enters on your left. Pass a former rice field. Climb wooden steps. Pass the preserve amphitheater.

1.4 Return to the parking area, completing the hike.

5 River Bluff Trail

Combine this fun, easy hike with a day of enjoying life on the Edisto River at Givhans Ferry State Park. Leave the park picnic area and dip into a ravine, then cruise along the bluffs of the Edisto River. Check out a tributary cascade before turning away to cruise flat woods. At trail's end turn around to see it from the opposite angle as you backtrack to the trailhead or make an optional loop using the park roads.

Distance: 2.0-mile there-and-back

Hiking time: 1 to 1.5 hours

Difficulty: Easy

Trail surface: Natural surface

Best season: Fall through spring

Other trail users: None

Canine compatibility: Leashed dogs permitted

Fees and permits: Entrance fee required

Schedule: 9 a.m.–sunset

Maps: Givhans Ferry State Park; USGS Maple Cane Swamp

Trail contacts: Givhans Ferry State Park, 746 Givhans Ferry Rd., Ridgeville, SC 29472, (843) 873-0692, southcarolinaparks .com

Finding the trailhead: From exit 199A on I-26 near Summerville, take US 17A south for 10 miles to SC 61 north toward Walterboro. Split away from US 17A on SC 61 north then drive for 8.0 miles to turn right on Givhans Ferry Road. Follow Givhans Ferry Road a short distance to turn left into the park. Follow the main park road to its end near Picnic Shelter #2. GPS trailhead coordinates: N33° 1.947', W80° 23.187'

The Hike

Givhans Ferry State Park has a historical bent to it. Originally the site of a 1700s ferry operated by Phillip Givhan,
the bluffs were developed by the Civilian Conservation
Corps into a state park during the 1930s, one of sixteen
CCC-developed state parks in South Carolina. The park
office and other buildings built at that time add a quaint
touch to the attractive natural setting. These limestone bluffs
are ecologically significant, hosting rare plants in the alkaline
soils, such as Carolina scaly stem and Southern shield fern.
The campground is located back from the Edisto but offers
fully equipped sites suitable for tents or RVs. Paddlers can
undertake a 6-mile float from Mars Old Field Ramp down
to the first-rate landing at Givhans Ferry State Park, viewing
the bluffs from the river along the way.

The River Bluff Trail offers a chance to walk along these
bluffs and wooded ravines that cut their way to the water. It
starts between the park's picnic shelters. You are already atop
the riverside bluff, so it is no surprise to dip into one of the
ecologically significant, wildflower-colored ravines that cut
into the bluff. Watch for exposed rock in the ravine.

Then you come along the mighty Edisto River. The
310-mile Edisto is free flowing from its origins down to the
Atlantic Ocean, and being the longest free-flowing blackwater river in the United States is its claim to fame. The river
basin is also the largest watershed contained entirely within
the boundaries of South Carolina. Its headwaters flow south
from the hills of Edgefield and Saluda Counties, working
southeast, picking up tributaries, forming the South Fork
Edisto and North Fork Edisto respectively. Here, the North
Fork flows around 100 miles, notably through the town of

Orangeburg, before merging with the South Fork Edisto, which has flowed a similar distance.

The two forks meet near Branchville, and together form the swift flow of black liquid. The river widens, becoming floatable year-round, and creates the boundary between Dorchester and Colleton Counties. After being fed by the wild waters of famed Four Holes Swamp, the Edisto passes the ecologically significant bluffs of Givhans Ferry State Park where this hike takes place, and where the river's south-easterly course was turned south by a long ago earthquake. (Some say the Ashley River follows the old course of the Edisto.) The Edisto aims for the Atlantic, becoming the tidal giant with which Charlestonians are familiar. The Edisto then splits around Edisto Island, before reaching the Atlantic Ocean.

Consider the river length when looking out on the Edisto. Just ahead is another ravine that sports a long angled cascade, arguably a waterfall, rare for the Lowcountry. After winter and spring rains, this rill can deliver quite a bit of whitewater. Turn away from the bluffs and cruise through gorgeous woods sprinkled in ferns. Walk alongside a wooded ravine to your right, then bridge its upper reaches. From there, enjoy a pleasant walk through upland flatwoods to emerge at a field and the main park road. This is where you must decide to either backtrack or follow the park road to the trailhead, completing the optional loop.

Miles and Directions

0.0 Join the River Bluff Trail at its signed entrance entering woods between park shelters #1 and #2. The natural-surface path stretches forth under magnolia, tall pines, and sweetgum.

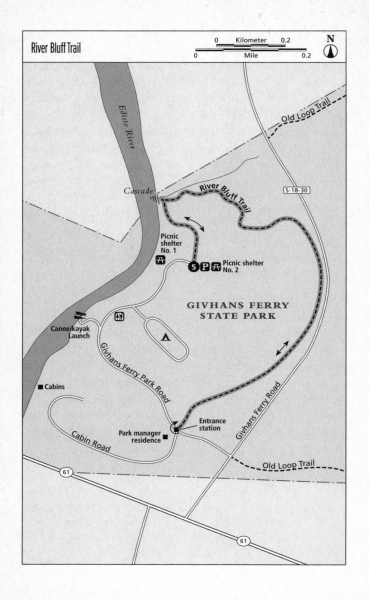

River Bluff Trail

0 Kilometer 0.2

0 Mile 0.2

N

Edisto River

Old Loop Trail

S-18-30

Cascade

River Bluff Trail

Picnic shelter No. 1

5 P Picnic shelter No. 2

GIVHANS FERRY STATE PARK

Canoe/kayak Launch

Givhans Ferry Park Road

Cabins

Cabin Road

Park manager residence

Entrance station

Givhans Ferry Road

Old Loop Trail

61

61

Quickly dip into a wooded wildflower-rich ravine. Then climb out.

0.1 Come alongside the river bluffs overlooking the Edisto. Come to another ravine, this one with a waterfall when flowing. Turn away from the river. Traverse rich woods with a wooded ravine to your right.

0.5 Cross a wooden bridge over the upper reaches of the ravine. Curve right, south, running parallel to Givhans Ferry Road, visible through the trees to your left. Cruise flatwoods.

1.0 Enter an open field to shortly reach the main park road near the entrance station. Turn around here to follow your path back to the trailhead. (***Option:*** Turn right onto the main park road, walk 0.6 mile past park facilities, and return to the trailhead, completing the loop option.)

2.0 Arrive back at the trailhead to complete the there-and-back version of the hike.

6 Old Loop Trail

This circuit hike wanders a little known lesser-visited parcel of Givhans Ferry State Park. Here, a doubletrack path circles the perimeter of upland forest where nature reigns and nothing but the natural world meets the eye. After starting at the park entrance at Givhans Ferry Road, you will circle the tract and return to Givhans Ferry Road. A walk along a mown strip beside Givhans Ferry Road leads you to the trailhead.

Distance: 5.1-mile loop
Hiking time: 2.5 to 3 hours
Difficulty: More challenging
Trail surface: Natural surface
Best season: Fall through spring
Other trail users: Bicyclers
Canine compatibility: Leashed dogs permitted
Fees and permits: Entrance fee required

Schedule: 9 a.m.–sunset
Maps: Givhans Ferry State Park; USGS Maple Cane Swamp, Ridgeville
Trail contacts: Givhans Ferry State Park, 746 Givhans Ferry Rd., Ridgeville, SC 29472, (843) 873-0692, southcarolinaparks .com

Finding the trailhead: From exit 199A on I-26 near Summerville, take US 17A south for 10 miles to SC 61 north toward Walterboro. Split away from US 17A on SC 61 north then drive for 8.0 miles to turn right on Givhans Ferry Road. Follow Givhans Ferry Road a short distance to turn left into the park. Park on the right in the field just after passing the entrance station. GPS trailhead coordinates: N33° 1.627', W80° 23.110'

The Hike

Sometimes when walking through seemingly pristine forests in local, state, or national parks, we imagine the lands being that way since time immemorial. That is certainly not the case here at Givhans Ferry State Park. While you walk the Old Loop Trail, the emphasis should be on the word *old*, for Givhans Ferry has been an integral part of South Carolina history. Situated along the banks of the river aboriginals called "Adusta" for its dark tint, the land along the Edisto became settled when 1700s colonists began spreading land-ward from Charleston. This bluff, at the river crossing of an Indian trail, was a logical homesite. White settlers followed this path linking Charleston to what became Augusta and Savannah, Georgia, and the Indian Trail became a regular road. By 1722, a fort stood on the bluff overlooking what was then called Worts Ferry. By the time of the Revolutionary War, Phillip Givhan had bought the land, using it for his home, a ferry operation, and a base from which to help supply American troops against the British.

Phillip Givhan and his family farmed this land and serviced the river crossing that was renamed Givhans Ferry. The land remained in family hands and the ferry stayed busier than ever. However, later heirs lost the land to debt. A fellow named George Rumph bought the land and ferry, but the state required Mr. Rumph to build a bridge over the Edisto. The bridge was in place by the 1850s but was burned by Union destruction specialist General Sherman during the Civil War. Today, SC 61 bridges the Edisto River at the ferry site.

Later, the property that is Givhans Ferry State Park changed hands a few times until it was bought by the city of

Charleston in 1899 as a potential source for the city's water supply. Nevertheless, it wasn't until the 1920s when Charleston tapped the Edisto, and even then it took them 9 years to build a 23-mile hand-excavated tunnel to a pumping station. The beginning of the tunnel is still on state park property and operates to this day.

However, in 1934, the city of Charleston conveyed the property to the state of South Carolina for the establishment of a state park and forest reserve (the forest reserve is where this hike takes place). However, there were two stipulations: If the land ever ceased to be a state park, it would revert to the possession of Charleston, and secondly that the state park never in any way pollute the Edisto River. Park facilities were immediately built by the Civilian Conservation Corps, including the ranger station that you see today. They also planted over 500 acres of the park in pine and hardwoods. The Old Loop Trail takes you through their handiwork, now grown up and matured.

Edisto State Park opened on June 1, 1937, and has operated ever since save for a few years during World War II. After the state established Edisto Beach State Park on Edisto Island, the park's name was changed to Givhans Ferry State Park. Charleston's search for drinking water would end up helping a favorite South Carolina state park come to be. Today we can hike the majestic woods and stand on the river bluffs, knowing a lot of history has taken place here.

This hike traverses woodlands and also passes within sight of wooded wetlands and swamps as it loops around the forest reserve that is the unsung part of Givhans Ferry State Park. The mostly grassy natural-surface path makes for easy hiking and is partly shaded. Parallel ditches run alongside the path.

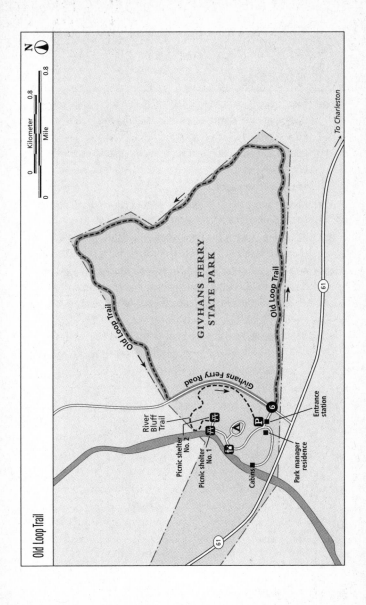

Old Loop Trail

Enjoy the sounds of nature. Look for deer and other wildlife along the way.

Miles and Directions

0.0 Leave east from Givhans Ferry Road as the Old Loop Trail passes around a pole gate. Enjoy a doubletrack path heading east under pines and oaks.

1.1 Pass a contemplation bench beside the trail. Continue eastbound.

1.7 The trail curves left, north.

1.9 Curve northeast, coming within sight of pine plantations, presenting a non-natural contrast to the state park.

3.3 Curve southwest, still on doubletrack, after passing through youngish forest.

4.4 Emerge on quiet Givhans Ferry Road. Look for a mown strip heading parallel to the road under a transmission line. It is a safer alternative to walking the road, which really is not dangerous.

5.1 Return to the park entrance, completing the loop and the hike.

7 Habitat Loop at Caw Caw Interpretive Center

The Habitat Loop at Caw Caw Interpretive Center uses a network of trails traversing a variety of habitats to deliver an all-encompassing overview of Lowcountry flora and fauna. The sheer number of trails will ensure repeat visits to this preserve. The trails are as varied as the terrain, using boardwalks over swamps, narrow natural-surface paths in deep woods, and open grassy tracks atop dikes.

Distance: 3.8-mile loop
Hiking time: 2 to 2.5 hours
Difficulty: Moderate
Trail surface: Natural surface and boardwalk
Best season: Fall through spring
Other trail users: None
Canine compatibility: Dogs not permitted
Fees and permits: Entrance fee required

Schedule: Tues–Sun 9 a.m.–5 p.m., closed Mon
Maps: Caw Caw Interpretive Center; USGS Ravenel
Trail contacts: Caw Caw Interpretive Center, 5200 Savannah Hwy., Highway 17 South, Ravenel, SC 29470, (843) 889-8898, ccprc.com

Finding the trailhead: From exit 212B on I-526 west near Charleston (the end of I-526 West), take Sam Rittenburg Boulevard a short distance to US 17. Turn right on US 17 south and follow it for 10 miles. The park entrance will be on your right. Continue on the park road to end at the visitor center. GPS trailhead coordinates: N32° 47.500', W80° 11.853'

The Hike

There are a total of 8 miles of trails at Caw Caw, which comes in at 654 acres. Two centuries ago the site was part of a 5,000-plus-acre rice plantation. A nature-oriented county park, Caw Caw offers extensive environmental education programs covering habitats, plants, rice cultivation, Gullah culture, and natural resource management, among other subjects. The visitor center is manned during park hours and the staff can answer other questions you may have. Water and restrooms are also available. Beyond that it is just you, nature, and a trail map.

The best way to experience Caw Caw is to follow the Habitat Loop, which incorporates the varied trails into one grand circuit, and is detailed on the park map. Interpretive kiosks are spread out along the trail system, adding an educational component to your hike.

The marshes and swamps of Caw Caw are managed to maximize conditions for wildlife. Water levels at the preserve are maintained by water control structures. On the Habitat Loop you will become very familiar with wetlands while taking the Georgia Pacific Swamp Boardwalk through cypress, maple, and gum trees of this seasonally inundated floodplain where cypress knees and palmetto grow in the shadow of the swamp giants.

The boardwalk ends and you trace a wide grassy road to the Laurel Hill Slave Settlement amid large live oaks. Nothing remains of the actual settlement, but the high ground under live oaks was home to African slaves while they worked the adjacent rice fields. The ground is the highest around and the oaks provided needed shade after working in the open rice fields. Restrooms are located near the settlement site.

Join a dike and open area on a grassy track heading toward the waterfowl area, now on the Waterfowl Trail. Swamp forest stands to your left, while open waters mixed with aquatic vegetation lie off to your right. The open wetlands are now managed for ducks instead of rice. Waterfowl will be seen here, in what were once agricultural fields. Open watery expanses, tidally influenced and brackish, border the left side of the trail. The right side is freshwater. The aforementioned water control structures also divide the fresh and saltwater areas. The tides push up nearby Wallace Creek.

The Maritime Forest Trail skirts a marsh in woods, then meets the Bottomland Hardwood Forest Trail in thick woods of hickory and oak. Pass some wild tea plants, leftover from when the area was a tea plantation. Later, vegetables were grown here, and you can still see the crop rows and shallow ditches made to drain the vegetable fields. The rest of the walk uses wide paths to loop you back to the visitor center.

Miles and Directions

0.0 Leave the walkway between the two buildings of the interpretive center, shortly reaching a trail junction. A trail leads to the right, reaching the rice field overlook boardwalk, which is worth a look. Imagine this open swamp once having been irrigated straight-lined rice fields. Leave the junction left, shortly intersecting the Swamp Sanctuary Trail and the Bottomland Hardwood Forest Trail. Begin the Habitat Loop by leaving right to cross a bridge over a strand of Caw Caw Swamp.

0.4 Head left on the Georgia Pacific Boardwalk, traversing a wooded swamp.

0.6 Leave right from the boardwalk toward Laurel Hill Settlement.

0.8 Pass the slave settlement site and keep straight, joining the Rice Fields Trail. Open onto dikes bordered by wetlands.

Habitat Loop at Caw Caw Interpretive Center

0 Kilometer 0.2

0 Mile 0.2

N

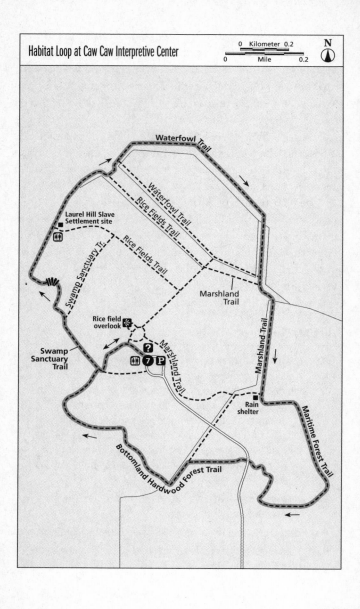

Waterfowl Trail

Waterfowl Trail

Rice Fields Trail

Laurel Hill Slave Settlement site

Swamp Sanctuary Tr.

Rice Fields Trail

Marshland Trail

Rice field overlook

Swamp Sanctuary Trail

?

7

P

Marshland Trail

Marshland Trail

Rain shelter

Maritime Forest Trail

Bottomland Hardwood Forest Trail

0.9 Leave left on the Waterfowl Trail, crossing a canal. Begin circling around marsh to your right.

1.6 Intersect the other end of the Waterfowl Trail coming in on your right. Stay left, atop a dike separating fresh and salt marshes. Pass a couple of water control structures, staying left, to join the wide Marshland Trail.

2.0 Come near a rain shelter, then head left on the singletrack Maritime Forest Trail. It enters woods that border a canal. Cedars are prevalent here, as the trail winds through palmetto. Views extend across the canal.

2.2 Join a doubletrack path leaving left.

2.3 Split right at a kiosk, back on singletrack path, joining the Bottomland Hardwood Forest Trail. This section can be mucky after rains, true bottomland.

2.8 Cross the park entrance road. The Bottomland Hardwood Forest Trail becomes doubletrack.

3.0 Stay left as a pink-blazed trail leaves right for the Marshland Trail. Continue in superlative, rich woodlands.

3.6 Complete the loop portion of the hike. Backtrack right toward the visitor center.

3.8 Return to the trailhead, completing the hike.

8 Dungannon Plantation Heritage Preserve

This hike presents an opportunity to walk through big woods to a wooded swamp, then a boardwalk and important South Carolina wood stork nesting site. Dungannon Plantation Heritage Preserve is also good for wildflowers. The walking is easy on mostly doubletrack paths. The final part uses a bridge and dike to pass through the wooded swamp before ending at the boardwalk. Your return trip can add variety via singletrack hiking trails.

Distance: 3.7-mile figure eight loop

Hiking time: 2 to 2.5 hours

Difficulty: Moderate

Trail surface: Natural surface and a little boardwalk

Best season: Fall through spring

Other trail users: None

Canine compatibility: Leashed dogs permitted

Fees and permits: None

Schedule: Sunrise–sunset

Maps: Dungannon Plantation Heritage Preserve; USGS Wadmalaw Island, Ravenel

Trail contacts: South Carolina Department of Natural Resources, Rembert C. Dennis Building, 1000 Assembly St., Columbia, SC 29201, (803) 734-3893, dnr.sc.gov/

Finding the trailhead: From exit 212B on I-526 west near Charleston (the end of I-526 West), take Sam Rittenburg Boulevard a short distance to US 17. Turn right on US 17 south and follow it for 7.3 miles to SC 162. Turn left on SC 162 and follow it for 3.9 miles to reach the trailhead on your right. Dungannon Heritage Preserve will be on your right. GPS trailhead coordinates: N32° 44.856', W80° 11.694'

The Hike

South Carolina has become an important wood stork breeding ground, as Florida's extensive wetlands continue to be diminished. The first wood stork nesting sites were found in South Carolina in 1981. The primary reason Dungannon Plantation was purchased by the state in 1995 was to provide wood stork nesting habitat. It is ironic to think that a swamp created by man for agricultural purposes some 200 years ago, to flood rice fields, has now become a breeding site for an endangered bird. Wood storks nest at Dungannon between April and July, sometimes starting earlier in spring. You should be able to see storks during that time here, however, the boardwalk itself may be closed then. In 2014, a total of 263 wood stork nests were counted inside the boundaries of Dungannon Plantation Heritage Preserve.

This swamp offers good nesting habitat for storks, which prefer living cypress trees 50 to 150 feet tall, with open water underneath. The rookery averages 110 nests per year, making it South Carolina's largest wood stork nesting area. The wood stork's federal status has been downgraded from endangered to threatened in 2014. This is good news, and they are definitely on the recovery track. In the US during the 1930s, between 15,000 and 20,000 breeding pairs of wood storks lived in the wild and by the late 1970s they had shrunk to around 2,500 total breeding pairs. Today, there are 1,500 to 2,500 wood stork nests in South Carolina alone.

The swamp is not only home for wood storks however. You may see alligators, egrets, wood ducks, blue herons, and other critters. Different seasons present not only varied wildlife observing opportunities, but also plant life, especially wildflowers, including the white swamp lilies, which light up the bottomland hardwood forest around Easter. This impoundment was once used to flood rice fields downstream from here. The DNR is also restoring natural habitats such as longleaf pine forests.

The hike traces the Main Trail, a doubletrack path, easterly along the edge of the preserve as it works around a swamp, formed when Mellichamp Creek was impounded long, long ago to provide manageable freshwater for the rice-growing operation of the Dungannon Plantation. This trail, along with the closed roads, is open to foot travel only, though the South Carolina DNR uses the roads for preserve management. After crossing an outflow of the swamp, use a dike to span the wetland.

After making it across the wetland, the Main Trail reaches an intersection. Here, the Main Trail heads north for the remote far end of the preserve, while our hike leaves left in flatwoods to soon reach the boardwalk and wood stork nesting site. A shady flat enhanced by a picnic table lies just before the boardwalk. Enjoy the boardwalk, scanning the area for wildlife. However, be apprised that the boardwalk is seasonally closed during nesting season, as the wood storks are very sensitive to human intrusion. On your return trip, take the alternate singletrack paths to see more of the forest and perhaps some of the five species of orchids that thrive in the preserve.

Miles and Directions

0.0 Leave the shaded Dungannon Preserve parking area in thick oak woods on a wide roadbed. Shortly leave right on the blue-blazed Main Trail, as the Yellow Trail and Red Trail 1 diverge.

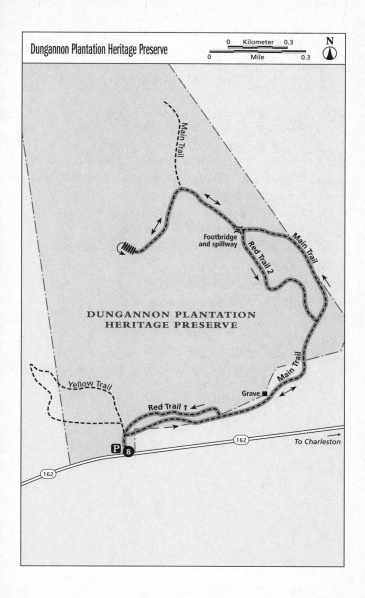

Dungannon Plantation Heritage Preserve

0   Kilometer   0.3

0   Mile   0.3

N

Main Trail

Footbridge
and spillway

Red Trail 2

Main Trail

DUNGANNON PLANTATION
HERITAGE PRESERVE

Yellow Trail

Red Trail 1

Grave

Main Trail

P 8

162

To Charleston

162

0.4 The Red Trail 1 comes in on your left. Keep straight on the Main Trail in pines and oaks. Houses and backyards on SC 162 are visible to your right.

0.6 Pass the lone grave of Matthew Sanford on your left. Curve left, northerly.

0.9 Singletrack Red Trail 2 leaves left and will be your return route. Keep straight on the Main Trail.

1.3 Drop off a hill and meet the other end of the Red Trail 2. Cross a spillway on a footbridge. Keep straight on a dike.

1.6 Head left toward the boardwalk and wood stork nesting area, as the Main Trail keeps straight.

1.8 Reach the boardwalk and stork area. Honor seasonal closures of the boardwalk. Backtrack.

2.3 Leave right on the Red Trail 2, rolling through big woods.

2.8 Rejoin the Main Trail.

3.3 Split right on singletrack Red Trail 1.

3.7 Return to the trailhead, completing the hike.

⑨ James Island County Park

This attractive park for active people sits on James Island, near the Stono River. Hikers enjoy a set of three interconnected paved pathways wandering the woods, fields, lakes, and marshes of this preserve. The hike starts near the park headquarters and runs along the main park lake. The loop then turns and circles through the north end of the park. It then comes along the marsh of James Island Creek. Enjoy aquatic views, working your way through park facilities to complete the circuit.

Distance: 3.4-mile loop
Hiking time: 2 to 2.5 hours
Difficulty: Easy
Trail surface: Asphalt
Best season: Year-round
Other trail users: Bicyclists
Canine compatibility: Leashed dogs permitted
Fees and permits: Entrance fee required

Schedule: Jan–Apr 8 a.m.–sunset, May–Labor Day 8 a.m.–8 p.m., Sept–Oct 8 a.m.–sunset, Nov–Dec 8 a.m.–5 p.m.
Maps: James Island County Park; USGS James Island
Trail contacts: James Island County Park, 871 Riverland Dr., Charleston, SC 29412, (843) 795-7275, ccprc.com

Finding the trailhead: From the intersection of US 17 and SC 171 in Charleston, take SC 171 south, Folly Beach Boulevard, for 2.1 miles, then turn right onto Central Park Road and follow it for 0.9 mile to Riverland Drive. Turn left on Riverland Drive to reach the park on your right after 0.5 mile. Enter the park, passing by the gatehouse, and continue 0.4 mile to the park center on your right, the same large parking area shared with Splash Zone Waterpark. GPS trailhead coordinates: N32° 44.092', W79° 59.416'

The Hike

This park operated by Charleston County has more facilities and features contained within its bounds than perhaps any other outdoor getaway in the greater Charleston area, and includes hiking trails. Visitors could come to James Island County Park for a week's vacation and never leave. How is that you ask? For starters, you can overnight in the campground, with a choice of spacious electric campsites for pop-ups and RVs, or more primitive sites for tent campers, all with access to showers. And if you don't feel like roughing it, stay at one of the park's cottages overlooking the marsh of James Island Creek. From there, you could head for Splash Zone Waterpark, with its aquatic offerings such as waterslides, a lazy river, fountains, and pools for those hot Lowcountry summer afternoons.

Or you could toss in a line from the fishing dock on James Island Creek. Alternatively, if you want to get on the water rent one of the park canoes, kayaks, or johnboats to explore the park lake (along which the trails travel). If you are outdoors oriented, as we hikers tend to be, you could test your skills on the tower-like climbing wall with challenges for all skill levels. Moreover, if you want to start out a little easier, try the bouldering wall. If it is a nice day head out for a round on the park's disc golf course, or take your dog to the large dog park that even has a beach and water access for the canine set. Still not enough? Visit the huge playground and watch your kids go wild, then afterwards cook lunch at one of the park shelters or picnic areas.

You can see it is no joke that visitors really could spend a week here and never get bored. The trail system is pretty neat, too. Both hikers and bicyclers explore the park and its three interconnected asphalt loops. There are many potential starting points, but the park center has a large parking area. You can pick up the Orange Trail near the bike and boat rental spot, then cruise along the park lake, watching pedal boaters try to keep their craft in line and avoid bumping into the shore.

From there, begin the loop portion of the hike, heading north through woods before coming near the primitive camping area and outdoor center. The loop then nears the cottages before turning along the woods bordering the marsh of James Island Creek. Soak in the best natural vistas as you look west toward the Stono River. From there, come near the surprisingly large playground and then make your final turns, passing the largest part of the park lake, before completing the impromptu tour of the bountiful facilities of James Island Park. After making your circuit, you will agree this place really is an all-inclusive outdoor vacation facility.

Miles and Directions

0.0 Leave from the boat and bike rental area behind the park center on the asphalt Orange/Blue Trail. Immediately cross a boardwalk over a wetland. Soon come alongside an arm of the park lake. Circle behind Splash Zone.

0.3 Reach a trail intersection. Head left with the Blue Trail. Turn north, parallel to James Island Parkway.

0.5 Cross James Island Parkway. Turn west, passing by the primitive campground.

0.9 Turn south and cross Marshview Circle the first of three times in succession.

1.1 Turn right onto the Green Trail. Travel pine, oak palmetto woods. James Island Creek marsh stretches west.

1.3 Cross Fishermans Way twice quickly.

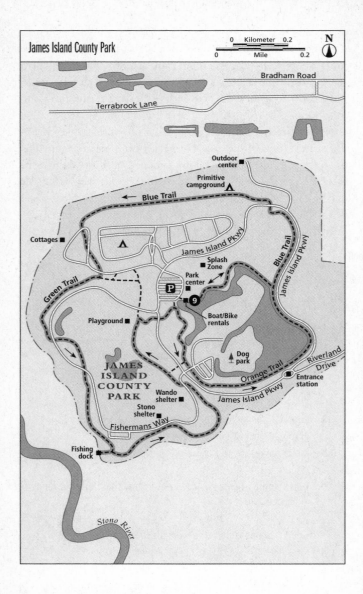

James Island County Park

	Kilometer	
0		0.2
0	Mile	0.2

N

Bradham Road

Terrabrook Lane

Outdoor center

Primitive campground

Blue Trail

Cottages

James Island Pkwy

Splash Zone

Park center

Blue Trail

James Island Pkwy

P

9

Green Trail

Boat/Bike rentals

Playground

Dog park

JAMES ISLAND COUNTY PARK

Orange Trail

Riverland Drive

Entrance station

Wando shelter

James Island Pkwy

Stono shelter

Fishermans Way

Fishing dock

Stono River

1.7 A spur leads right to the fishing dock and a view. Turn east in canopied woodland.

2.1 Cross Fishermans Way a final time. Ahead, a spur leads right toward the dog park parking area. Stay straight. Pass a pond and reach the large playground.

2.4 Turn right onto the Orange/Blue Trail. Cross James Island Parkway.

2.5 Return to the park center parking area, but turn right onto the Orange Trail. Head south, passing near the dog park parking area.

2.8 Come alongside the park lake.

3.1 Complete the loop portion of the hike. Head left on the Blue/Orange Trail, backtracking.

3.4 Return to the trailhead, completing the hike.

10 Charles Towne Landing

Come see where South Carolina was born and where the first Charleston colonists set up in 1670, at a preserved state historic site. The hike leads you first to the Animal Forest, where a variety of creatures from bears to bison to bobcats are ensconced in habitats, along with farm animals. From there you will head out to Albemarle Point, the site of Charleston's original settlement, viewing historic sites and absorbing interpretive information. See the ship *Adventure* on Old Towne Creek. On your way back view the Legare–Waring House and Mrs. Waring's Garden.

Distance: 2.6-mile loop with spur
Hiking time: 1.5 to 2 hours
Difficulty: Easy
Trail surface: Asphalt and natural surface
Best season: Year-round
Other trail users: Bicyclists
Canine compatibility: Leashed dogs permitted, except in Animal Forest
Fees and permits: Entrance fee required

Schedule: 9 a.m.–5 p.m. daily, closed Christmas Eve and Christmas Day
Maps: Charles Towne Landing; USGS Charleston
Trail contacts: Charles Towne Landing State Historic Site, 1500 Old Towne Rd., Charleston, SC 29407, (843) 852-4200, south carolinaparks.com

Finding the trailhead: From exit 216A on I-26 north of downtown Charleston, take SC 7 south for 1.8 miles to veer left onto SC 171, Old Towne Road, at a traffic light. Stay on SC 171 for 0.5 mile to turn left into the state historic site. The hike starts from the rear of the visitor center. GPS trailhead coordinates: N32° 48.401', W79° 59.210'

The Hike

Imagine embarking on the ultimate move—across the Atlantic Ocean to a little-known continent, to settle in untamed lands inhabited by natives about which you knew nothing, not to mention knowing little of the land upon which you were to settle. And that is exactly what happened to a group of 120 colonists who settled at Albemarle Point, near the confluence of what became known as Old Towne Creek and the Ashley River. Though this spot was hampered because it lacked a deep-water port, it was more defensible than what became the town of Charleston we see today across the Ashley River. Nevertheless, for 9 years the colonists of Charles Towne Landing carved out a life on this spot.

Thus became the first European settlement in South Carolina, and today is one of just a few preserved original settlement sites existing in the United States. And today you can come and tour it. The 634-acre park, complemented with 80 acres of gardens, presents a picture of the past that covers not only the time of the colonists, but also of aboriginal South Carolinians, African slaves, the antebellum plantation period, and the later residents of the peninsula who occupied what is known as the Legare-Waring House.

Your historical hike starts at the visitor center and museum, which gives you an overview of what took place at Charles Towne Landing. The hike then cruises by an aboriginal ceremonial site, then a slave cemetery before delving into natural history at the Animal Forest. Here, you can check out red wolves, bears, bison, and otters in outdoor habitats. Also, view the domestic livestock as well. Kids of all ages love to see the animals up close.

After leaving the Animal Forest, you will pass by the noble statue of Cassique, an Indian who helped the colonists. Pass by the Horry-Lucas House ruins, where a pre–Civil War plantation once stood. Next, enter the original settlement area. Though little remains from the actual settlement, archaeologists have figured out the basic layout and lifeways of Charles Towne. See the Common House, the defensive cannons, and "the stocks" where those who ran afoul of the law were sent.

Stop by the water and see the ship *Adventure*. They sometimes fire off the cannons, a sight to see. There is also a recreated shipbuilding area. The archaeology exhibits explain how the area was systematically dug for clues to the past. Then you move on to another place and period. In spring, the gardens of the Legare-Waring House, a popular site for weddings and special events, will color the grounds in pink, purple, and red, completing the experience.

Miles and Directions

0.0 After passing through the visitor center, leave east, crossing a boardwalk above the nearby pond. Join the signed History Trail, an asphalt track.

0.1 Reach a trail intersection. Head left on the Animal Forest Trail. Pass by the African American Cemetery, then come to the concentration of animals. The paths split, heading to the various exhibits. Backtrack after viewing the animals.

1.2 Rejoin the History Trail after visiting the critters. Pass by the statue of Cassique, then come to the circular walk around the Horry-Lucas homesite ruins. From here, stay left with the history walk as it cuts through the Palisade Wall and enters the Original Settlement, with multiple exhibits.

1.8 Come to the ship *Adventure*, a replica 1700s sailing vessel, docked in Old Towne Creek. The History Trail turns back

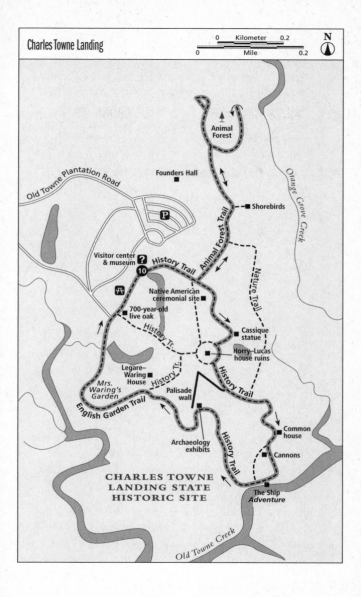

Charles Towne Landing

Kilometer 0 — 0.2
Mile 0 — 0.2

N

Old Towne Plantation Road

Founders Hall

P

Visitor center & museum

History Trail

Animal Forest Trail

Animal Forest

Shorebirds

Orange Grove Creek

Nature Trail

Native American ceremonial site

700-year-old live oak

History Tr.

Cassique statue

Horry–Lucas house ruins

Legare–Waring House

History Tr.

Mrs. Waring's Garden

English Garden Trail

Palisade wall

History Trail

Archaeology exhibits

Common house

Cannons

History Trail

CHARLES TOWNE LANDING STATE HISTORIC SITE

The Ship Adventure

Old Towne Creek

north, bridging a wetland on a boardwalk. Ahead, pass the archaeology exhibits, by a line of live oaks.

2.2 Reach a trail intersection. The Legare-Waring House is to your right. Head left on the English Garden Trail, passing under widespread live oaks and azaleas, hibiscus, and camellia.

2.5 Meet the other end of the History Trail after passing by a pond. Look right for the 700-year-old live oak. It was here during the time Charles Towne was settled. Keep straight toward the visitor center, nearing a picnic area.

2.6 Return to the visitor center, completing the hike.

11 Palmetto Islands County Park

Situated on a mix of wooded islands and cordgrass marshes bordered by tidal streams, Palmetto Islands County Park presents a series of interconnected natural–surface and asphalt trails exploring what once was an aboriginal seasonal camp, plantation, brick–making area, and now county park. Today, you can hike amid maritime woods, along cordgrass marsh, and visit Nature Island. The walk continues to an elevated observation tower where you can look over the Wando River basin and other tidal waterways. Beyond that, the trek passes near picnic areas, fishing docks, and the balance of park offerings.

Distance: 3.5-mile multi-loop
Hiking time: 2 to 2.5 hours
Difficulty: Moderate
Trail surface: Natural surface and asphalt
Best season: Year-round
Other trail users: Bicyclists
Canine compatibility: Leashed dogs permitted
Fees and permits: Entrance fee required

Schedule: Jan–Apr 8 a.m.–sunset, May–Labor Day 8 a.m.–8 p.m., Sept–Dec 8 a.m.–sunset
Maps: Palmetto Islands County Park; USGS Fort Moultrie
Trail contacts: Palmetto Islands County Park, 444 Needlerush Pkwy., Mount Pleasant, SC 29464, (843) 884-0832, ccprc.com

Finding the trailhead: From exit 28 on I-526 north of Mount Pleasant, take Long Point Road east for 1.7 miles to Needlerush Parkway. Turn left on Needlerush Parkway and follow it 1.3 miles to enter Palmetto Islands County Park. Upon entering the park, pass the entrance gate then take your first right and then take a second immediate right into the dog park parking area. GPS trailhead coordinates: N32° 51.732', W79° 49.902'

The Hike

The park trail system and facilities are inextricably intertwined underneath a lot of forest, making the numerous roads, trails, and facilities seem confusing upon your first visit here. This is understandable, since there is an abundance of both trails and amenities at this park situated along Horlbeck Creek and its tidal tributaries, marshes, and smaller islands. Despite the beauty of this 943-acre park, its biggest draw is Splash Island, a waterpark with a body flume, sprays and geysers, a water ride, and a pool manned by lifeguards. Maybe you can go swimming after your hike . . .

The park also has boat and bike rentals, a large playground, multiple fishing docks, a kayak launch, and numerous picnic areas and shelters. The dog park is also a big draw and you start your hike there. The hike settles alongside a cordgrass marsh in surprisingly attractive woods of live oak, palm, cedar, and yaupon. Extensive views stretch out across the marsh, dotted with the Palmetto Islands, for which the park is named. Ahead, you will visit one of these Palmetto Islands, now named Nature Island. A long boardwalk spans the marsh, linking Nature Island to the main park area. The name is appropriate since this isle has been left in its natural state, overlain only with trails. The trip out to Nature Island allows you to visit uninterrupted forest, and features an extensive westerly view to the Wando River.

Aboriginals use to stay on islands such as this during the summer, harvesting shellfish and other foods from the nearby waterways. They also enjoyed sea breezes that kept things relatively cool. In fall, they left, to not only get away from the worst of the hurricane season, but also reap the inland bounty, from meaty mammals to succulent berries.

After leaving Nature Island, skirt around the north side of the park, enjoying more views of the cordgrass marshes and tidal creeks. The park observation tower allows an elevated vista that stretches to the horizon, and is a true highlight of the hike. The second part of the trek heads over to Horlbeck Creek, a large tidal waterway. You cruise along the edge of this stream, passing fishing docks. The loop curves out to a peninsula and then makes a series of loops linked by the Marsh Trail and the Bicycle Trail.

Miles and Directions

0.0 After parking in the dog park lot, join the paved Bicycle Trail leaving north from the parking area. Go just a short distance then turn left on the yellow-blazed Osprey Trail. The first part is paved, then it crosses the road to the Splash Island parking, then becomes a natural-surface trail, sometimes overlain with gravel. Pass a ranger residence on your left then come alongside marsh. Hike through maritime hardwoods of palm, live oak, and cedar with the marsh to your left and the parking area to your right.

0.3 Reach a trail intersection. Head left onto a boardwalk toward Nature Island. Cross a cordgrass marsh.

0.4 Head left on the loop portion of the Nature Island Trail. Walk under pines, palms and wax myrtle. Stay left, passing a shortcut.

0.8 Stay left again to join the spur with a westerly view of the Wando River. Continue the loop, passing the other end of a shortcut.

1.1 Complete the loop on Nature Island. Backtrack over the boardwalk toward the main park.

Palmetto Islands County Park

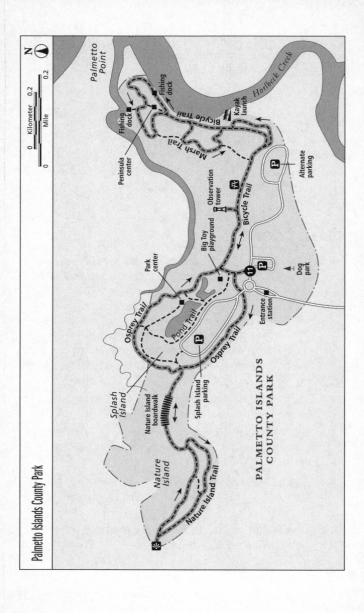

PALMETTO ISLANDS
COUNTY PARK

1.2   Head left on natural-surface Osprey Trail. Walk the margin of wood and marsh, with the paved Bicycle Trail and Splash Island to your right.

1.5   Open onto a view and connector to the Pond Trail. Keep straight on the Osprey Trail. Pass near the park office, joining the Bicycle Trail.

1.7   Pass the trail leading right to the dog park. Keep straight, walking under a transmission line.

1.8   Come to the observation tower. Grab a view then keep east on the Bicycle Trail.

2.0   Pass the Marsh Trail leaving left. Stay right, then join another part of the Marsh Trail. Curve north along Horlbeck Creek.

2.2   Come near the kayak launch. Stay right, briefly joining the Bicycle Trail only to spur away.

2.4   Pass near the Peninsula Center and fishing dock. Curve around the peninsula, passing another fishing dock.

2.7   Stay left as a branch of the Marsh Trail splits right as a boardwalk. Rejoin the Bicycle Trail.

2.8   Split right, making a second loop on the Marsh Trail. Rejoin the Bicycle Trail, backtracking.

3.5   Return to the trailhead after backtracking on the Bicycle Trail.

12 **Wannamaker County Park**

This North Charleston preserve presents a series of interconnected natural-surface nature trails and paved paths you can
use to cobble together a woodsy loop near Goose Creek.
The number of trail intersections may seem daunting during
your first visit. Nevertheless, the following loop will give
you a good overview of the park, from the backwoods near
Goose Creek and the north end of the park to the developed
areas near the waterpark, the park lake, playground, and park
center.

Distance: 2.3-mile loop
Hiking time: 1.5 to 2 hours
Difficulty: Easy
Trail surface: Asphalt and natu-
ral surface
Best season: Year-round
Other trail users: Bicyclists,
joggers
Canine compatibility: Leashed
dogs permitted
Fees and permits: Entrance fee
required

Schedule: Jan–Apr 8 a.m.–
sunset, May–Labor Day 8 a.m.–8
p.m., Sept–Dec 8 a.m.–sunset
Maps: Wannamaker County Park;
USGS Ladson
Trail contacts: North Charleston
Wannamaker County Park, 8888
University Blvd., North Charleston,
SC 29406, (843) 572-7275,
ccprc.com

Finding the trailhead: From exit 205B on I-26 north of Charleston,
take US 78 east for 0.9 mile to the park entrance on your left. Once
past the entrance gate, follow the signs to the park center. GPS trailhead coordinates: N32° 58.621', W80° 3.094'

The Hike

The county of Charleston has developed a formula for its parks: include something for everyone. Wannamaker County Park is no exception. The biggest draw is Whirlin' Waters Adventure Waterpark, a 15-acre water play facility that features a huge wave pool, a racing waterslide, a crazy tubular waterslide, an aquatic treehouse, and a lazy river flow for less adventurous waterpark visitors. Whirlin' Waters is open during the warm season and really does pack 'em in.

However, the balance of the 1,015-acre park is nature-based, with more traditional park facilities, including picnic areas, picnic shelters, a lake, and a sizable playground. It does have a sprinkler water play area that pales in comparison to the aquatic offerings at Whirlin' Waters.

And of course it has trails. Wannamaker County Park offers a color-coded network of paved and natural-surface trails that wander throughout the preserve. These trails are well marked and maintained and there is a map at almost every intersection, helping you keep apprised of your whereabouts, because despite the setup, the sheer number of trail intersections can be confusing to first-time visitors (and second-time visitors). But you will also notice lots of regulars coming here to hit the trails for their daily exercise, developing routes of their own. Just try to look like you know your position while casually consulting the intersection trail maps.

This route takes full advantage of the trail network, making the largest loop possible within the bounds of Wannamaker. It joins the asphalt Blue Trail and heads toward the park entrance, where you pick up the natural-surface Red Trail. Traverse alluring forest en route to Goose Creek. Here, the sloping terrain drops to a wetland along Goose Creek.

You then join shorter nature trails on the edge of wooded swamp. Come near the park lake via a paved path, then the final part of the hike uses the natural-surface Peach Trail to complete the loop and return you to the trailhead. As mentioned, don't be surprised if you have to consult the maps at the trail intersections. Finally, focus on enjoying the woods and wildlife of the park and you will surely have a successful hike at Wannamaker County Park.

Miles and Directions

0.0 As you face the park center, leave right on the asphalt path, passing the playground on your left and the parking area on your right. Reach a trail intersection at the edge of the parking lot. Here, the natural-surface Peach Trail leaves left, while the asphalt Blue Trail leaves right. Follow the Blue Trail across the road to overflow parking and toward the dog park.

0.2 Cross the road leading to the Whirlin' Waters parking lot. Curve right and continue in woods, paralleling the park entrance road.

0.4 Cross the park entrance road within sight of the entrance station. Join the natural-surface Red Trail, leading back into woods. Head under pines, magnolia, and oaks with an understory of beard cane and yaupon. Watch for blooming wild azaleas in spring. This is the most remote part of the park. Contemplation benches are scattered in the woods here.

1.0 Go over a pair of boardwalk bridges, then reach a trail intersection. Stay left with the natural-surface Pink Trail as the Red Trail heads to alternate parking. Continue in gently rolling woods with a few more live oaks thrown into the mix.

1.1 The Dark Purple Trail leaves right. You keep straight on the Pink Trail. Walk just a short distance and reach another intersection. Stay straight on the Pink Trail as the Orange Trail leads right. Ahead, come within sight of the paved Purple

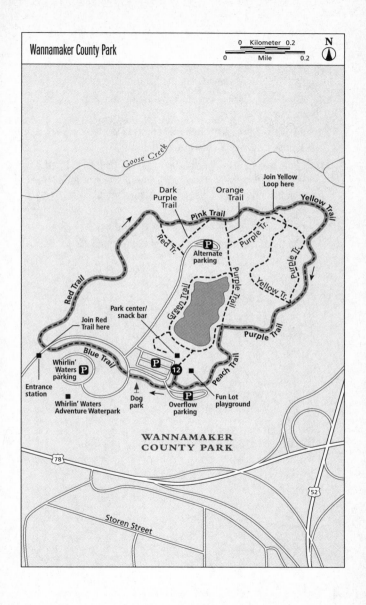

Trail as you slip between the swamp to your left and the Purple Trail to your right.

1.3 Meet the Yellow Loop. Stay left, joining the natural-surface path as it skirts the edge of the park.

1.6 Come very near the paved Purple Trail again. Stay on natural-surface path.

1.7 Intersect the paved Purple Trail and take it left, heading southwest. Make an easy woodland walk.

2.0 Come to a four-way intersection near the park lake. Head left on the natural-surface Peach Trail, walking south. Ahead, skirt behind the park playground. Come near the overflow parking area.

2.3 Complete the loop. You are within sight of the park center and the trailhead. Stroll a few feet north, completing the hike.

13 Old Santee Canal Park

History and wildlife buffs will love this walk. Start at the informative park interpretive center, then walk the wetlands and bluffs of Biggin Creek, viewing a former limestone kiln and the Old Santee Canal, finished in 1800. Cruise by the modern Tailrace Canal before returning to Biggin Creek and visit observation decks where birds and alligators can be seen. Finally, visit Stony Landing House, a historic home over-looking waters below.

Distance: 2.0-mile loop
Hiking time: 1 to 2 hours
Difficulty: Easy
Trail surface: Natural surface, boardwalk
Best season: Year-round
Other trail users: None
Canine compatibility: Leashed dogs permitted outside of buildings

Fees and permits: Entrance fee required
Schedule: 9 a.m.–5 p.m. daily
Maps: Old Santee Canal Park; USGS Cordesville
Trail contacts: Old Santee Canal Park, 900 Stony Landing Dr., Moncks Corner, SC 29461, (843) 899-5200, oldsanteecanal.org

Finding the trailhead: From Charleston, take US 52 west to Moncks Corner and US 52 Bypass. Here, join US 52 Bypass, keeping straight. US 52 Bypass is also called R. C. Dennis Boulevard. Follow US 52 Bypass/R. C. Dennis Boulevard for 1 mile to reach Stony Landing Road. Turn right on Stony Landing Road and follow it for 0.6 mile to enter the park. Continue past the entrance station to reach the interpretive center. Address is 900 Stony Landing Drive. GPS trailhead coordinates: N33° 4.213', W79° 31.191'

The Hike

While South Carolina was but an English colony, Charleston traders sought a way for crops to be shipped from the Midlands down to Charleston, avoiding a dangerous trip to and then along the coast from the mouth of the Santee River to Charleston. If the Santee and Cooper Rivers could be connected, then goods could be safely floated directly to Charleston, which was good for the farmers of the Midlands and good for the traders of South Carolina's shipping center. The Santee Canal Company set about building a canal with locks linking the Santee and Cooper Rivers. The 22-mile canal took 7 years to finish, and in 1800 began five decades in existence. Cotton and other products were towed by mules and pushed by men.

The nineteenth century moved on. Railroads replaced canals for product transportation. The canal was abandoned, then mostly submerged under Lake Moultrie. However, the canal here remains intact. Add the historic Stony Landing House, the modern Tailrace Canal, and the waters of Biggin Creek all protected as a park and you have a fine destination.

The hike begins behind the interpretive center. Enter the interpretive center through a replica of a canal lock made of brick. These locks were used to raise and lower flatboats as they traveled along the Old Santee Canal. Inside are historic and interpretive displays that are well worth your time, and you can learn about the trials of building this historic canal using the tools of the day. Natural history information is displayed as well.

Leave the interpretive center on a boardwalk, then a hiking trail and dry land. Pass an old limestone kiln and alongside limestone bluffs, rare for these parts. The trail continues up the left bank of Biggin Creek, in the margin between the limestone bluff and the creek to your right. Surprisingly, the trail climbs steps up to the top of the bluff, back down, then back up again and down one more time to cross the Old Santee Canal. Next, curve alongside the Tailrace Canal, the modern connector between what is now Lake Moultrie and the Cooper River. The Old Santee Canal was 35 feet wide and 5.5 feet deep, and is minute in comparison to the Tailrace Canal alongside which the trail travels. A hill, likely from fill dirt from the Tailrace Canal, pinches you in from the right. Reach the first of several spur trails leading away from the canal, over the hill and back down to bird-watching decks on Biggin Creek.

Ahead, bridge the outflow of Biggin Creek, where it meets the Tailrace Canal and the Cooper River. The path opens onto the lawn of the Stony Landing House, circa 1843. This landing was an important trading location for South Carolina dating back to the 1730s, and where the first successful underwater attack submarine, the CSS *Little David*, was built. The house and grounds are well preserved, and the house is filled with period furnishings and open for tours. Leave the grounds and return to the parking area, passing the interpretive center to your right.

Miles and Directions

0.0   Leave from the lower rear of the interpretive center and head left on a boardwalk. Quickly pass a boardwalk leaving north across Biggin Creek. Stay straight and pass the canoe launch. Continue past a shortcut to the interpretive center parking lot, and a limestone bluff and kiln, now on the Alligator Loop.

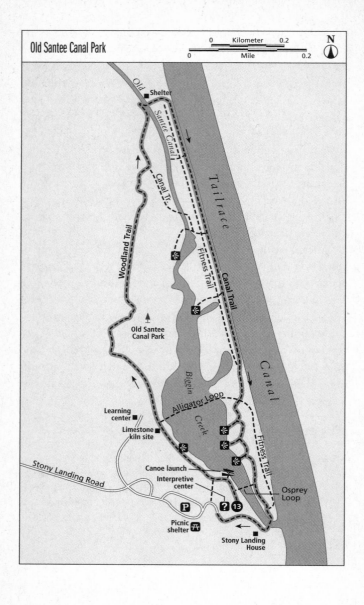

0.2 Here, a boardwalk leads right, across Biggin Creek and shortcuts the hike. A viewing platform is dead ahead and overlooks Biggin Creek. Keep left here on the Woodland Trail.

0.8 The Canal Trail enters right. Join it and emerge where Biggin Creek and the Old Santee Canal meet. A trail to an observation point continues up the left side of the canal. Cross a boardwalk across the canal and through a rain shelter. Turn south along the Tailrace Canal. The Fitness Trail runs parallel to you on a hill.

1.5 Reach an intersection where the Fitness Trail leaves left but you head right, down a small hill, rejoining the Alligator Loop. Don't take the loop across the creek but stay on the north bank, visiting three separate observation decks.

1.8 The Osprey Loop leaves right across the creek back to the interpretive center. Stay left.

1.9 The Fitness Trail comes in on the left. Stay right crossing the outflow of Biggin Creek. Rise to circle behind Stony Landing House, then head toward the interpretive center.

2.0 Return to the interpretive center, completing the hike.

14 Turkey Creek Hike

This backcountry hike traverses deep woods in Francis Marion National Forest along one of the most scenic freshwater creeks in the region. Walk in a lush valley where piney slopes transition to swamp hardwoods, exuding everywhere-you-look beauty. South Carolina's master path—the Palmetto Trail—is your conduit through this forested hinterland where bridges and boardwalks aid your passage through wildflower-rich wetlands.

Distance: 5.4-mile there-and-back
Hiking time: 2.5 to 3 hours
Difficulty: Moderate
Trail surface: Natural surface
Best season: Fall through spring
Other trail users: Bicyclists
Canine compatibility: Leashed dogs permitted
Fees and permits: None

Schedule: 24/7/365
Maps: Swamp Fox Passage of the Palmetto Trail, Section 2, Section 3; USGS Bethera, Huger
Trail contacts: Francis Marion National Forest, 2967 Steed Creek Rd., Huger, SC 29450, (843) 336-3248, www.fs.usda .gov/main/scnfs/

Finding the trailhead: From exit 23 on I-526 northeast of downtown Charleston, take Clements Ferry Road north for 7.7 miles to turn left on Reflectance Drive (there will be a sign to turn left to access SC 41 north here). Follow Reflectance Drive for 0.6 mile to reach SC 41 and a flashing light. Turn left here and follow SC 41 north for 13.7 miles to where the Palmetto Trail crosses SC 41, which will be 0.2 mile after the bridge over Turkey Creek. *Note:* The parking area on the west side of SC 41 is small, so be considerate. GPS trailhead coordinates: N33° 7.986', W79° 46.993'

The Hike

The Palmetto Trail, which this hike uses, travels the entire length of South Carolina from the mountains to the sea. The Palmetto Trail is divided into sections known as passages. The 45-mile Swamp Fox Passage of the Palmetto Trail travels its entire distance through the Francis Marion National Forest. The Swamp Fox Passage is named after the American Revolutionary War hero Francis Marion. He repeatedly harassed British forces and then fled to the coastal wetlands, only to attack again. And for his cunning ways, Francis Marion was dubbed the "Swamp Fox."

The original portion of what was called the Swamp Fox Trail was finished in 1968 by Boy Scouts. The Swamp Fox Trail then became part of the Palmetto Trail, and ultimately was dubbed the Swamp Fox Passage of the Palmetto Trail. The Swamp Fox Passage leaves Lake Moultrie and winds through longleaf pine woods, hardwood floodplains, evergreen shrub bogs, and blackwater swamps on the way to its end at US 17.

Beech trees, abundant on this hike, are easy to identify. Their smooth gray trunks make them stand out in the forest, as the carved trees along this trail testify. Many woodland walkers simply cannot resist the flat surface of the beech—it seems a tablet for a handy pocketknife. Pick up a beech leaf from the forest floor. They are generally 2 to 4 inches long with sharply toothed edges, dark green on top and lighter underneath. In fall, they turn a yellowish golden brown. After the leaves fall from the beech, notice the buds of next year's leaves. The half-inch buds resemble a mini-cigar. Come spring, these buds will unfurl, becoming next year's leaves.

Beechnuts are an important food for wildlife, from bears to mice to deer, and birds from ducks to blue jays. Critters break apart the burr-covered shell to reach the nutrient-rich treat. For man, the wood of beech trees is used for everything from flooring to railroad ties to charcoal.

This part of the Palmetto Trail runs alongside Turkey Creek, running underneath vast stands of beech and tulip trees, with Turkey Creek or its tributaries never distant. Civilization seems distant and nature sounds fill the air. Cruise east in the attractive Turkey Creek valley in the hilly margin between wetland and upland, occasionally spanning small branches on bridges in the bottomlands. Hike through the sloping valley that creates a transitional environment, adding more vegetational variety than most sections of the Palmetto Trail. Some viney sections of forest seem junglesque. Fall is a good time to hike this section of the Palmetto, with the plentiful hardwoods turning vibrant colors and the pathway at its driest.

Toward the end, the Palmetto Trail uses long narrow boardwalk bridges to span wetlands, then climbs from the Turkey Creek bottoms into upland pines. A few large loblolly pines stand out en route to FR 166, Conifer Road. This is a good place to turn around. From FR 166, the Swamp Fox Passage of the Palmetto Trail continues south and east for US 17.

Miles and Directions

0.0   Leave east from SC 41 on the Swamp Fox Passage of the Palmetto Trail. The trail quickly enters pine woods and spans a tributary of Turkey Creek on a footbridge. Walk under rolling pines, oaks, and copious beech trees.

0.5   Cross a boardwalk over another tributary of Turkey Creek.

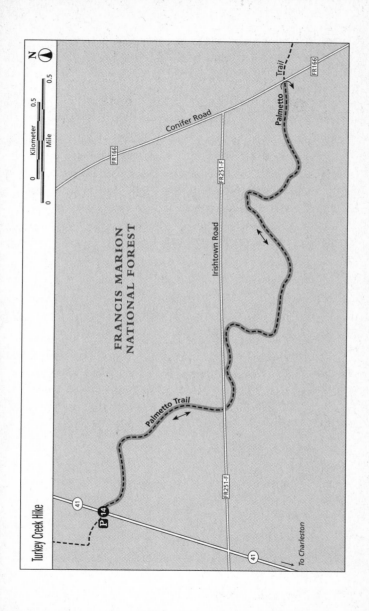

Turkey Creek Hike

FRANCIS MARION
NATIONAL FOREST

Palmetto Trail

Palmetto Trail

Conifer Road

Irishtown Road

FR166

FR166

FR251-F

FR251-F

P 14

41

41

To Charleston

N

Kilometer   0.5

0   0.5

Mile

0.8 Reach and cross FR 251-F, Irishtown Road. The trail then turns easterly in bottomlands with a swampy section of Turkey Creek to your right and FR 251-F to your left.

1.2 Cross a tributary by culvert. Turn away from FR 251-F.

1.4 Cross wetlands on occasional slender boardwalk bridges. Look for wildflowers in spring.

2.0 Bridge another tributary of Turkey Creek. Turn down along the stream you just crossed. Cross more long boardwalk bridges.

2.2 Climb away from the creekside bottoms. Pass underneath pines. Look for occasional bigger pines.

2.7 Reach FR 166, Conifer Road. This is a good place to turn around. Backtrack on the Palmetto Trail.

5.4 Return to SC 41, completing the hike.

15 Carolina Bay Hike

This hike starts at a primitive national forest campground and follows South Carolina's master path—the Palmetto Trail—through upland woods, then joins an old logging railroad grade, passing through a Carolina bay, one of the unusual oval–shaped wetlands extending through the Carolinas and beyond to New Jersey and down to Florida. After passing through the bay, you then traverse wooded swampland, still on the railroad grade. The hike then emerges at a forest road that makes for a good place to turn around.

Distance: 3.8-mile there-and-back
Hiking time: 2 to 2.5 hours
Difficulty: Moderate
Trail surface: Natural surface
Best season: Fall through spring
Other trail users: Bicyclists
Canine compatibility: Leashed dogs permitted
Fees and permits: None

Schedule: 24/7/365
Maps: Swamp Fox Passage of the Palmetto Trail, Section 1; USGS Ocean Bay
Trail contacts: Francis Marion National Forest, 2967 Steed Creek Rd., Huger, SC 29450, (843) 336-3248, www.fs.usda .gov/main/scnfs/

Finding the trailhead: From exit 23 on I-526 northeast of downtown Charleston, take Clements Ferry Road north for 7.7 miles to turn left on Reflectance Drive (there will be a sign to turn left to access SC 41 north here). Follow Reflectance Drive for 0.6 mile to reach SC 41 and a flashing light. Stay straight here, joining Halfway Creek Road. Follow Halfway Creek Road for 11.1 miles to the right turn into Halfway Creek Trail Camp. Follow the forest road a short distance to dead-end at a small auto turnaround and the trailhead. GPS trailhead coordinates: N33° 3.343', W79° 41.729'

The Hike

Carolina bays are unexplained natural phenomena occurring in the Lowcountry, among other places, on the Atlantic coastal plain. A Carolina bay is an elliptical or oval depression, ranging from an open lake to a thickly vegetated seasonal wetland, varying in size from over 1 acre to over 1,000 acres. These depressions, sometimes grouped together, fill with rainwater during winter and spring, then dry out as fall comes on. The depth of water determines the plants and animals that occupy a Carolina bay.

Sounds just like some regular old swamp, doesn't it? Not so fast, junior ranger. Carolina bays are unique and unexplained for the following reasons: They are always elliptical or oval in shape and their axes always orient northwest to southeast. They always have raised sand rims and depressed interior surfaces with the soils of the bay differing from the surrounding soils. To confuse things further, these bays are not named bays because they are filled with water, but because they are often bordered with bay trees.

As seen from the air, these Carolina bays truly stand out. Over 200 Carolina bays lie in South Carolina, with over two dozen within the bounds of the Francis Marion National Forest. Many of these unique wetlands have been filled in, dug out, or otherwise altered. Intact bays are fire dependent to preserve their ecosystem of not only bay trees, but also fetterbush, pond cypress, and the carnivorous pitcher plant.

The origin of Carolina bays is a mystery. Every theory as to how these unusual wetlands came to be is flawed. Some people think it was from upwelling of water when the continents were being formed, or from wind blowing water around after the last major glaciation, or even a giant meteor shower pocking the earth!

No matter how they came to be, they are an important part of the Lowcountry's greater ecosystem. This hike takes you by one of these unusual wetlands. First, start at primitive Halfway Creek Trail Camp, an auto-accessible designated camping area with no amenities. Even the pump well has been capped. However, the Swamp Fox Passage of the Palmetto Trail passes directly through the camp. You pick up the Palmetto Trail, traversing young hardwoods that soon give way to pines. The Palmetto Trail runs parallel to Halfway Creek Road before curving southeasterly, where it picks up an arrow-straight former logging grade.

Compared to the surrounding terrain, the logging tram is dry. As you follow it, look for old railroad ties embedded in the ground, as well as roots running perpendicular to the trail, as they grew along now rotted ties. It is here the trail passes alongside a Carolina bay. From the path, the bay looks simply like a low brushy wetland. This bay is a thick shrubby one, also known as pocosin. The word meaning "swamp on a hill" is credited to Algonquin Indians. These pocosins are important places for amphibians, reptiles, and wading birds.

As you continue southeasterly, the trail leaves the Carolina bay and passes through more typical Lowcountry swamp forest as well as piney woodlands before emerging at FR 224, which is a good place to turn around. Pass through the Carolina bay a second time before returning to Halfway Creek Trail Camp.

Miles and Directions

0.0 With your back to the parking area, walk a short connector path to an open grassy area and the Palmetto Trail. Head

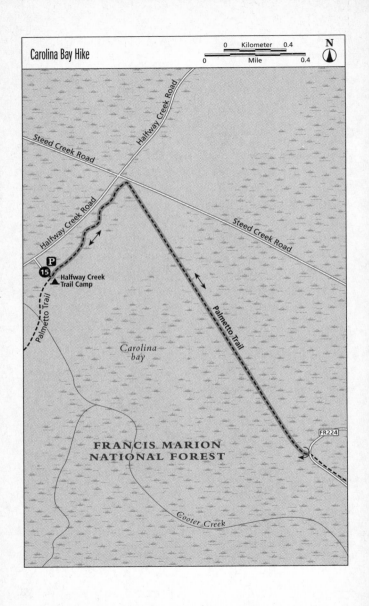

Carolina Bay Hike

Kilometer

Mile

N

Steed Creek Road

Halfway Creek Road

Halfway Creek Road

Steed Creek Road

P

15

Halfway Creek
Trail Camp

Palmetto Trail

Palmetto Trail

Carolina
bay

FR224

FRANCIS MARION
NATIONAL FOREST

Cooter Creek

left, northwest, away from the capped pump well of Halfway Creek Trail Camp. Enter young hardwoods. Just ahead, cross a little ditch and enter a pine grove.

0.5 Turn southeast in turkey oaks after passing an alternate parking area near the intersection of Halfway Creek Road and Steed Creek Road. The Palmetto Trail joins an old logging railroad grade. Descend gently, Look for railroad ties.

0.8 Come along the Carolina bay to your right. Pass through wetlands.

1.5 Cross a closed forest road, now a linear wildlife clearing. Ahead, cross a wooden hiker bridge.

1.9 Reach FR 224. The Palmetto Trail leaves right on the forest road. Turn around and backtrack.

3.8 Return to the trailhead, completing the hike.

16 Ion Swamp Circuit

This is your chance to walk through a place that is much more water than land without getting your feet wet! Make a loop through Ion Swamp, where dark waters lie below tall trees, where birds call and other creatures lurk in the distance. Yet, you will see evidence of when this back of beyond was once a working rice plantation, with canals and dikes still visible. Much of your walking will be atop low, irregular dikes from the 1700s, left to time and the elements. Interpretive signage enhances the experience.

Distance: 2.0-mile balloon loop
Hiking time: 1 to 1.5 hours
Difficulty: Easy
Trail surface: Natural surface
Best season: Fall through spring
Other trail users: None
Canine compatibility: Leashed dogs permitted
Fees and permits: None

Schedule: 24/7/365
Maps: Ion Swamp Interpretive Trail; USGS Ocean Bay
Trail contacts: Francis Marion National Forest, 2967 Steed Creek Rd., Huger, SC 29450, (843) 336-3248, www.fs.usda .gov/main/scnfs/

Finding the trailhead: From exit 30 on I-526 in Mount Pleasant, take US 17 north for 16 miles to Ion Swamp Road, FR 226 (if you reach the Sewee Visitor & Environmental Center on your right you have gone 0.2 mile too far). Turn left onto FR 226 and follow the gravel road for 2.4 miles and the trailhead will be on your left. GPS trailhead coordinates: N33° 0.278', W79° 40.961'

The Hike

When you explore Ion Swamp, the thick forests belie its previous incarnation as a rice plantation, a place cleared in the 1700s to plant what became South Carolina's "white gold." The swamp was named for Colonel Jacob I'on, who owned the land in the early 1800s. Later, when official US Geological Survey maps were made, the name was mistakenly changed to Iron Swamp and eventually back to Ion Swamp. Name aside, the swamp became part of Wytheywood and Clayfield Plantations. A trailside interpretive sign states it all, giving the recipe for a 1700s South Carolina rice plantation:

> *Traditional Rice Dish*
>
> *1. Clear swamp of all trees by hand*
> *2. Dig ditches and build banks with hand tools*
> *3. Build wooden floodgates to control drainage and water flow to rice fields*
> *4. Cultivate rice by hand using mules wearing special rawhide boots to keep them from sinking in the mud*
> *5. Perform the above tasks in extreme heat and humidity and periods of heavy rain, thick clouds of mosquitoes and possibly with swamp fever, a.k.a. malaria.*

While exploring the swamp you will also see metal relics leftover from when the area was further altered after the plantation days. Nowadays, a system of metal water control structures has been installed to manage water levels for wildlife. In plantation days, these water control structures were wooden dams with boards laid vertically and added or removed to change water levels. Today, metal pipes and gates are used, and the pipes are opened or closed with hand cranks resembling steering wheels.

The hike turns along Wytheywood Canal. The canal served two functions. First, it was used to irrigate the rice fields. Second, it was used to move push pole–driven boats loaded with rice down the 7-mile hand-dug canal to the Wando River and on down the Wando to Charleston to be sold. Slaves dug the canals, cleared the land, and built the levees upon which you walk today. Consider the physical toils that have taken place here, as you lightly toil on your walk, in a place now reverted to the howling wilderness, where time and the healing hand of nature, with a little help from man, has turned this from a sun-scorched level field, laced with dikes, to a wooded wetland where nature's beasts from the reptilian alligator to singing warblers now thrive.

Nowadays, trees line the canal, and grow in the middle of it. It has partly filled up with forest debris and couldn't be floated today. Willow trees grow alongside the dikes. Alligators may be seen during warmer weather. Bring insect repellent if hiking this trail in the heat. Tupelo trees, also known as gum trees, complement the cypress. Maples, sweetgum, and oaks occupy higher ground. While completing the circuit, look for grids in the land and waters, evidence of the old rice days. The last part of the walk traces the Wytheywood Canal a final time before completing the loop portion of the hike. From there backtrack to the trailhead.

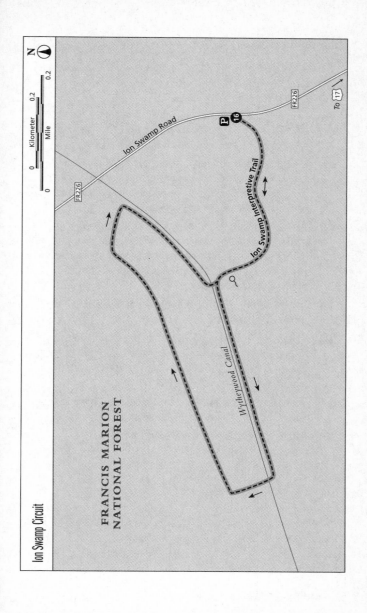

Ion Swamp Circuit

FRANCIS MARION NATIONAL FOREST

N

Kilometer

Mile

0   0.2

0   0.2

Ion Swamp Road

FR226

FR226

To 17

16

P

Ion Swamp Interpretive Trail

Wytherwood Canal

Miles and Directions

0.0   Leave the trailhead on a narrow foot trail beneath sweetgum, oak, pine, and bay trees. Cross a short boardwalk to join a doubletrack path leaving right.

0.4   Pass a spring on trail left, then reach the loop portion of the hike and the Wytheywood Canal. Turn left here, with the canal to your right and wide swamp off to your left.

0.8   The trail reaches a metal water control structure. Here, the loop crosses the canal and turns right, leaving the Wytheywood Canal to parallel another canal. Cypress knees rising on the trail can trip the unwary walker.

0.9   The trail turns again and passes through nearly pure red maple stands. While walking the wooded wetlands, search out the grid pattern of the rice fields. A keen eye can see the elevated lines dividing the lower wetter areas, despite the passage of three centuries.

1.3   The trail turns again, then crosses a boardwalk over a particularly wet section.

1.4   Cross the old Wytheywood Canal for the second time on a bridge. The trail then parallels the Wytheywood Canal again. Wood duck nesting boxes are scattered in the woods in great numbers.

1.6   Span another boardwalk just before completing the loop portion of the hike. Backtrack to the trailhead.

2.0   Return to the trailhead, completing the hike.

17 Nebo Nature Trail

This hike encompasses many highlights in a short distance. First, start at the Sewee Visitor Center, where you can learn a lot about the Lowcountry's natural history. From there, take a boardwalk past a pond, then come to a red wolf viewing area, where you can see the canines in action. The trail then passes through wooded swamp and coastal woodlands before circling around more ponds. Finally, the path returns to the visitor center, where you can learn a little bit more about this part of the world.

Distance: 1.6-mile balloon loop

Hiking time: About 1 hour

Difficulty: Easy

Trail surface: Natural surface and boardwalk

Best season: Fall through spring

Other trail users: None

Canine compatibility: Dogs not allowed

Fees and permits: None

Schedule: Wed–Sat 9 a.m.–5 p.m.

Maps: Sewee Visitor and Environmental Education Center; USGS Sewee Bay

Trail contacts: Sewee Visitor and Environmental Education Center, 5821 US Highway 17 North, Awendaw, SC 29429, (843) 928-3368, www.fs.usda.gov/main/scnfs/

Finding the trailhead: From exit 30 on I-526 in Mount Pleasant, take US 17 north for 16.2 miles to turn right into the Sewee Visitor and Environmental Center. The address is 5821 US Highway 17 North. **Note:** The gates of the visitor center close promptly at 5 p.m., and if your car is left here you will be ticketed. GPS trailhead coordinates: N33° 0.064', W79° 36.559'

The Hike

At the Sewee Visitor and Environmental Center, you can enhance your hike with environmental education, learning about the wonderful wildlands that stretch throughout the Lowcountry of South Carolina of which Charleston is the epicenter. Although the Charleston area was the first place settled in the Palmetto State, vast stretches of nearby protected places remain in a relatively undisturbed state, from the islands and marshes of Cape Romain National Wildlife Refuge to the extensive woodlands of the Francis Marion National Forest to additional state parks and preserves, as well as county parks. However, nowhere will you get a more comprehensive collection of natural history than at Sewee Visitor and Environmental Center. Jointly operated by Francis Marion National Forest and Cape Romain National Wildlife Refuge, the visitor center not only has the Nebo Nature Trail for us hikers, but it also has exhibits detailing the ecosystems of the wildlife refuge and national forest and primary habitats of the Lowcountry, extending from barrier islands along the coast to freshwater swamps and hilltop hardwood forests well inland.

Before your hike take time to explore the visitor center. You have to walk through it anyway to get to the trailhead. The displays not only detail the natural history but also the people and lifeways of pre-Columbian South Carolina. Check out the video on the local lands and the recreational opportunities therein. Next, grab a trail map and head out the back door. View the butterfly garden, then jump onto the Nebo Nature Trail.

The loop trail first cruises behind a pond where you might see an alligator. It then heads to the red wolf habitat, where these fascinating canines live. Though they are fenced in, they do have a large area to roam. You will learn more seeing them live in person than by other means.

Continue on a boardwalk through swamp forest before joining a natural-surface trail. It eventually leads to old Nebo Pit Road, a now-closed auto access to former phosphate mines that are filled with water and present fishing and waterfowl viewing opportunities. Here you can see reclamation firsthand, viewing how wise land management can turn a former mine area into an enhanced wildlife habitat. After circling the ponds, return toward the visitor center on the old mine access road, coming near the Cape Romain National Wildlife Refuge headquarters building before turning past one more pond, this one quite small, and reaching the visitor center. After your walk, head back inside. You may have more natural history questions to be answered, and the Sewee Visitor and Environmental Education Center is a good place for that.

Miles and Directions

0.0 Leave left from the back door of the visitor center, after inspecting the butterfly garden. Pick up a boardwalk and the Nebo Nature Trail. Bridge a waterway, curve left, and cruise along a pond, absorbing interpretive information.

0.1 A spur trail leads left to the parking area. Turn right here, still on boardwalk.

0.2 Come to the spur leading left to the red wolf habitat. Walk to the viewing area overlooking the enclosure. Return to the main loop, traversing a wetland on boardwalk.

0.4 The boardwalk ends. Veer right on a wide, natural-surface track under pines.

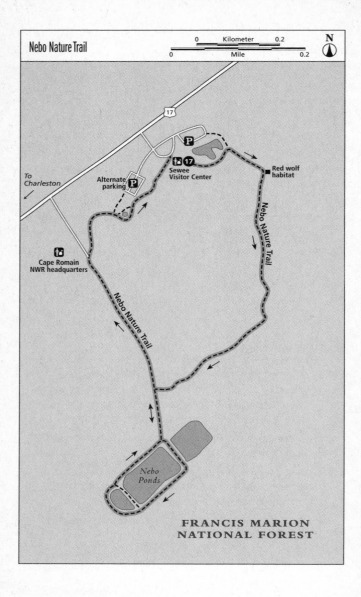

Nebo Nature Trail

0   Kilometer   0.2

0   Mile   0.2

N

17

P

To
Charleston

Alternate
parking

P

Sewee
17 Visitor Center

Red wolf
habitat

Nebo Nature Trail

Cape Romain
NWR headquarters

Nebo Nature Trail

Nebo
Ponds

FRANCIS MARION
NATIONAL FOREST

0.6 Come to old Nebo Pit Road. Head left toward the Nebo Ponds.

0.7 Reach the Nebo Ponds and a wildlife viewing blind. Stay left here, splitting between two ponds that are popular fishing spots, as wildlife personnel has placed fish attractors into the water. Begin circling clockwise along the shore of the ponds.

0.8 A shortcut between two ponds leaves right. Stay left, circling around the outermost pond.

1.0 Complete the loop of the Nebo Ponds. Head north, back-tracking on old Nebo Pit Road.

1.1 Keep straight, passing the earlier hiked segment of the Nebo Nature Trail.

1.3 Curve right near the Cape Romain National Wildlife Refuge headquarters.

1.4 A spur leads left to a large parking area. Stay right here, curving past a small pond. Emerge from the woods and join a sidewalk heading toward the front of the visitor center.

1.6 Return to the visitor center, completing the walk.

18 Sewee Shell Ring Interpretive Trail

You can see a lot of history on this walk. Explore two relics of history, the 4,000-year-old Sewee Shell Ring and a 600-year-old clam shell midden, both vestiges of previous cultures. The shell ring is considered ceremonial, while the clam midden is from harvesting nearby tidal waters for food. The loop hike also travels through tall woods, along a salt marsh and by rare shell mound vegetation.

Distance: 1.0-mile balloon loop
Hiking time: About 1 hour
Difficulty: Easy
Trail surface: Natural surface and boardwalk
Best season: Fall through spring
Other trail users: None
Canine compatibility: Leashed dogs permitted
Fees and permits: None

Schedule: 24/7/365
Maps: Sewee Shell Ring Interpretive Trail; USGS Awendaw, Bull Island
Trail contacts: Francis Marion National Forest, 2967 Steed Creek Rd., Huger, SC 29450, (843) 336-3248, www.fs.usda .gov/main/scnfs/

Finding the trailhead: From exit 30 on I-526 in Mount Pleasant, take US 17 north for 17.1 miles to turn right on Doar Road. Pass the Awendaw water tower and Awendaw town hall, following Doar Road for 2.1 miles to Salt Pond Road, FR 243. Turn right on FR 243 and follow it 0.3 mile to the trailhead on your right. GPS trailhead coordinates: N33° 0.064', W79° 36.559'

The Hike

Imagine exploring South Carolina's coastline and coming upon a circular shell ring approximately 3 to 10 feet high and 225 feet in diameter. If you are like early colonial South Carolinians, you might think it was a product of the local Sewee Indians, who roamed coastal Carolina in the 1600s. After all, the Sewee utilized the resources of the coastline, eating shellfish such as clams and oysters, as well as finny fish. In addition, you know there is a clamshell midden in close proximity to the strange, circular shell ring with the flat center. Why wouldn't it be the Sewee? A midden is a trash pile left over from consuming shellfish. However the nearby clamshell midden is just that—an unsystematic, haphazard pile of shells rather than the specific circular form of the nearby but ultimately misnamed Sewee Shell Ring.

Not only was the Sewee Shell Ring not made by the Sewee Indians, archaeologists have found out that the Sewee Shell Ring is over 4,000 years old, preceding the Sewee by thousands of years! No one knows the name of the aboriginals who left the Sewee Shell Ring, but we do know a bit about them. It seems their shell ring evolved from a simple shell midden piled up from their nearby dwellings. Later, the aboriginals moved from the area, but not before re-forming their midden from a simple pile to circular ring with the open plaza that we see today. This ring was then used in feasts, ceremonies, and as an everyday gathering place.

The Sewee Shell Ring is the northernmost of these ceremonial rings that stretch along the coastline from here to Florida. Many of them have been torn apart or otherwise reused without consideration for their archaeological worth. That is what makes this spot so valuable. The hike also takes you to the shell midden actually left by the Sewee Indians. The hike starts in young spindly woods then takes you into rich maritime coastal forest and the edge of a marshy estuary to reach the Sewee Shell Ring. There, join a boardwalk to walk along a portion of the ring, hollow in the center. At this point you also may see some of the unusual plants that grow along heaps of shells. The calcium seeped from the shells into the ground alters the soil, changing its composition, allowing rare and unusual plants to thrive, such as shell-mound buckthorn, Spanish bayonet, and coral bean.

Beyond the Sewee Shell Ring, the hike leads along the edge of cordgrass marsh through maritime woods to visit the relatively new Sewee shell midden. After all, it is only 600 years old and is primarily clamshells. A spur trail leads out to the mound. You then start working your way back to the trailhead, passing through youngish woods that were completely flattened when Hurricane Hugo passed through in 1989. Even though they seem fledgling and gangling, imagine the area a few decades back, when there was nothing but fallen trunks and post-hurricane debris.

Miles and Directions

0.0 Leave the wooded Salt Pond Road trailhead, heading south into thick, cool forest of live and willow oak, pignut hickory, and magnolia. Swampy, wooded wetlands stretch out beyond.

0.1 Come to the loop portion of the walk. Note the interpretive signage detailing natural and human history of the locale. The forest becomes young and spindly, a result of Hurricane Hugo.

0.4 Reach a trail junction. The path going left shortcuts the loop and misses the historical sites. Instead, stay right and shortly come to a second intersection. You are on the edge of the marsh. Here, stay right and join the boardwalk circling around the south side of the Sewee Shell Ring. Note views near and far and the circular ceremonial site, plus unusual

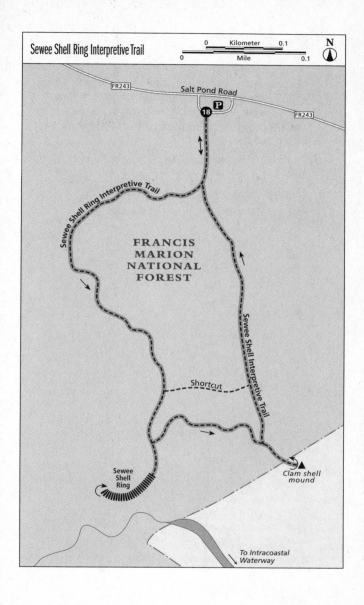

Sewee Shell Ring Interpretive Trail

0   Kilometer   0.1

0   Mile   0.1

N

FR243

Salt Pond Road

FR243

18 P

Sewee Shell Ring Interpretive Trail

FRANCIS
MARION
NATIONAL
FOREST

Sewee Shell Interpretive Trail

Shortcut

Sewee
Shell
Ring

Clam shell
mound

To Intracoastal
Waterway

plants. Backtrack from the boardwalk's end and continue the loop, passing along the shore.

0.7 Come to another intersection after passing a monstrous live oak and plentiful palms. Here, take the spur right that leads a short piece out to the 600-year-old shell mound. This seems more a scattered pile of food refuse, but calcified soil here also alters vegetation patterns, thus more cedars. Backtrack to the main loop.

0.8 Pass the shortcut and keep straight, traversing young woods again.

0.9 Complete the loop portion of the hike. Backtrack.

1.0 Return to the trailhead, completing the hike.

19 Awendaw Creek Hike

Walk along a scenic tidal stream ensconced in maritime forestlands. Start on a bluff overlooking Awendaw Creek and a bordering tidal marsh, then wind in and out of woods, occasionally crossing boardwalks over open marshes. Farther on, extensive vistas of the Intracoastal Waterway and beyond to Cape Romain National Wildlife Refuge are revealed. End at a spot called Walnut Grove, where massive live oaks enhance the palms and other waterside woodland.

Distance: 4.2-mile there-and-back
Hiking time: 2 to 2.5 hours
Difficulty: Moderate
Trail surface: Natural surface
Best season: Fall through spring
Other trail users: Bicyclers
Canine compatibility: Leashed dogs permitted

Fees and permits: None
Schedule: 24/7/365
Maps: Awendaw Passage of the Palmetto Trail; USGS Awendaw
Trail contacts: Francis Marion National Forest, 2967 Steed Creek Rd., Huger, SC 29450, (843) 336-3248, www.fs.usda .gov/main/scnfs/

Finding the trailhead: From exit 30 on I-526 in Mount Pleasant, follow US 17 north for 22 miles to Rosa Green Street. Look for the sign stating "Awendaw Creek Canoe Launch." Turn right on Rosa Green Street and follow it for a half-mile to reach the trailhead on your left. GPS trailhead coordinates: N33° 1.815', W79° 36.194'

The Hike

This hike encompasses a portion of the Awendaw Passage of the Palmetto Trail, widely regarded as one of the prettiest portions of the Palmetto Trail, which runs the length of

South Carolina from the Atlantic Ocean to the Southern Appalachians. When finished, the Palmetto Trail will stretch 450 miles. For more information on the Palmetto Trail and your role in completing the path, please visit www.palmetto conservation.org.

This hike covers only a couple of miles of the Palmetto Trail, but it is an outstanding section. For starters, the walk traverses a rare parcel of coastal national forestland that is eye-pleasing to the extreme. The trailhead is also the starting point for one of South Carolina's better paddles—Awendaw Creek. An elaborate paddler-only handicap-accessible launch has been built at this trailhead. Go ahead, walk down to the water, and view Awendaw Creek up close before your hike. Check the tides. Are they going in or out? Peer across the cordgrass marsh to the far side of Awendaw Creek. Wooded bluffs rise that way too. Beyond lies Cape Romain and the Atlantic Ocean.

The hike heads downstream along Awendaw Creek. You are already on elevated bluff, adding to the panoramic pos- sibilities. The scenery in the near is excellent as well, as you walk on a sandy, needle-carpeted trail shaded by maritime woodland of cedar, pine, and live oaks. Wax myrtle, holly, and yaupon add more evergreen to the ecosystem. At points, you will turn away from Awendaw Creek then cross cordgrass marshes via wide boardwalks and span other smaller, wooded streamlets on little bridges. The bridges over the cordgrass marshes provide still more vista opportunities. Take a minute to peer into the water and see what aquatic life lies in the brackish flats. Ideally located contemplation benches avail opportunities to relax and soak in the scenery.

The trail continues an alternating pattern of coming alongside Awendaw Creek and its bluffs then turning away from the edge of the creek, working around tributaries, then returning to the bluff. The interchanging open marsh and dense woods creates a striking contrast. Watch for shorebirds in the marshes.

The lower wetter parts of the trail may be rooty. Watch your feet. Ahead, the forest becomes dotted with palms, adding a tropical touch. Live oaks increase in number, too. The Palmetto Trail bridges a deep tidal stream at the so-called Time Warner Bridge, where a large wetland extends landward. Once again the trail returns to the edge of the marsh. Scan the horizon for boats here, as the Intracoastal Waterway is close. Admire the nearly vertical live oaks overhanging the marsh, their sturdy limbs winding above the water. Ahead, the Palmetto Trail crosses a bridge and turns north, landward into pines, leaving the marsh. This is a good place to turn around. It is a little less than 2 miles farther to Buck Hall and the Palmetto Trail's eastern terminus.

Miles and Directions

0.0 Leave the Awendaw Creek Canoe Launch and trailhead atop a bluff, overlooking the paddler dock below. Cruise a 4-foot-wide well-maintained trail. Head east under cedars, loblolly pines, and oaks. Views stretch toward the Atlantic, down the flats of Awendaw Creek.

0.2 Cross a boardwalk bridge over cordgrass marsh after turning away from Awendaw Creek. Reenter woods, crossing more minor streamlets on small bridges.

0.3 Cross a long boardwalk bridge over a small serpentine tidal creek bounded by vegetated marsh. Reenter lush maritime forest then head for a bluff.

0.4 Come to a contemplation bench at the edge of a bluff overlooking a bend of Awendaw Creek. Keep east, turning away

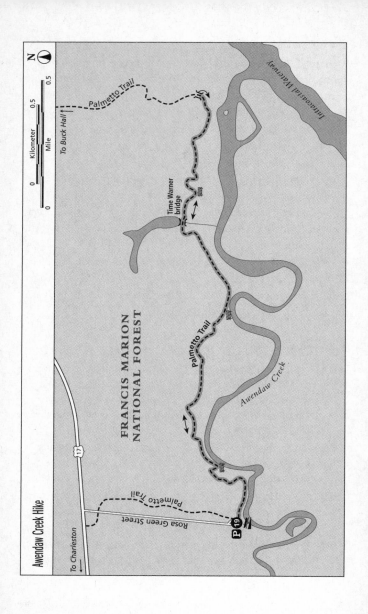

Awendaw Creek Hike

FRANCIS MARION
NATIONAL FOREST

Palmetto Trail

Palmetto Trail

Palmetto Trail

Time Warner
bridge

Awendaw Creek

Intracoastal Waterway

Rosa Green Street

P 19

To Buck Hall

To Charleston

17

N

Kilometer   0.5

Mile

0   0.5

from the bluff. More intermittent streambeds cross the Palmetto Trail.

0.9 Emerge at a transmission line clearing. Turn left along the clearing, then reenter woods, leaving right. Soon rejoin the bluff along Awendaw Creek.

1.1 Cross a wide boardwalk bridge over marsh. Return to Awendaw Creek.

1.3 Walk across another wide boardwalk over wetland. Straddle the margin between cordgrass flats and maritime woods.

1.6 Bridge a tidal stream on a span with handrails. This is known as the Time Warner Bridge. A lake-like wetland opens to your left, while cordgrass marsh and Awendaw Creek are to your right.

1.7 Come to a contemplation bench situated in a live oak copse. The bench overlooks open marsh.

1.8 Cross another boardwalk bridge over cordgrass flats. Reenter woods with more palms and live oaks. Watch for live oaks hanging over the marsh, and massive live oaks shading the trail. Look for exposed shells when the tide is lower. In the distance, scope for boats plying the Intracoastal Waterway.

2.1 Reach another bridge in a spot known as Walnut Grove. This is a good place to turn around, as the trail leaves Awendaw Creek for good.

4.2 Return to the trailhead, completing the hike.

20 Trails of South Tibwin

This hike offers some of the finest views in the Lowcountry. The terrain through which you walk is the former South Tibwin Plantation, now part of the Francis Marion National Forest. Traverse thick woods and then come upon a fresh-water impoundment, good for birding. Work your way along dikes to the edge of Tibwin Creek, where marshes and woodlands stretch to the horizon, presenting natural vistas seldom seen in this part of the country. The views get even better when you come within sight of the Intracoastal Waterway, gaining views to the Atlantic Ocean and beyond, sans civilization.

Distance: 3.5-mile loop
Hiking time: 1.5 to 2 hours
Difficulty: Moderate
Trail surface: Natural surface
Best season: Year-round
Other trail users: Bicyclers
Canine compatibility: Leashed dogs permitted
Fees and permits: None

Schedule: 24/7/365
Maps: South Tibwin Hiking Trails; USGS Awendaw
Trail contacts: Francis Marion National Forest, 2967 Steed Creek Rd., Huger, SC 29450, (843) 336-3248, www.fs.usda .gov/main/scnfs/

Finding the trailhead: From exit 30 on I-526 in Mount Pleasant, follow US 17 north for 27 miles to the South Tibwin entrance, FR 245, on your right. This is 3.1 miles beyond Buck Hall Recreation Area. Parking is immediately after the turn. GPS trailhead coordinates: N33° 4.213', W79° 31.191'

The Hike

The land that once was South Tibwin Plantation is now a large tract of transitional terrain, where the tall pine forests of the inland Lowcountry morph to freshwater and brackish wetlands, ultimately linking to the Atlantic Ocean. The US Forest Service acquired South Tibwin in 1996 as part of its efforts to create a natural as possible transition area from land to sea. Not only is it an important wildlife corridor and habitat area, the tract also houses the most significant historic building in the entire 260,000-acre Francis Marion National Forest, the South Tibwin Plantation manor. This two-story wooden building was built in 1803. South Tibwin Plantation came to be in 1705 when an English land grant was given to one Captain John Collins. In the 1700s, it continued to pass through his family but was ultimately acquired by William Matthews, who built the historic house and land. Originally, the manor was closer to the ocean but was later moved back from the waterfront after a hurricane threatened the home. South Tibwin continued to be inhabited and the land worked in rice, Sea Island cotton, and potatoes.

By the late 1930s, South Tibwin seems to have been abandoned, and the home fell into disrepair. Interestingly, Henry Ford purchased a rice mill from South Tibwin Plantation, and it is still on display in Dearborn, Michigan. The rice days are long gone, but wildlife thrives on the big tract. Furthermore, interest has grown in preserving the plantation house, partly due to its significance to the area. Once a historic building is lost, it is gone forever. Hurricane Hugo tore the roof off the house, but the US Forest Service replaced the roof and stabilized the building. In 2014, the house was stabilized again, as the front porch was pulling away from the front of the structure. More funds are being sought to complete a restoration of the house, which is estimated to cost around $500,000.

You will not see the plantation house on your hike. It is across Tibwin Creek. However, you will view a variety of woods, waters, marshes and even out to the Intracoastal Waterway and Cape Romain National Wildlife Refuge. Take note, the trails are not named but are merely a network of tracks. The hike joins a closed forest road then loops past a couple of Forest Service houses, before curving along a freshwater impoundment. Walk along the pond then turn alongside tidal Tibwin Creek, where cordgrass marshes and natural coastal scenes please the eye. The trails are double-track, allowing you to look around, instead of watching every footfall.

More views open as you come closer to the coast and are walking atop elevated open dikes that avail views in all directions, including seaward. These are some of the best panoramas in the Lowcountry. More ponds are out here and are important bird nesting areas. Thus, some trails are closed seasonally. The last part of the hike leads through freshwater swamps and back to upland forest and the trailhead.

Miles and Directions

0.0 Leave the parking area on US 17, heading south on gated FR 245. Just ahead, a trail enters on the right. Keep straight on the forest road.

0.2 Reach an intersection in woods near a pair of houses, national forest buildings. Head left, passing between a house on your right and one on your left, northeasterly.

0.3 A lesser-used doubletrack heads left, but you stay right.

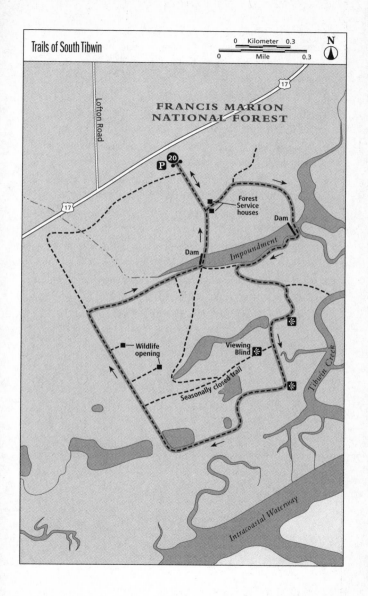

Trails of South Tibwin

0 — Kilometer — 0.3
0 — Mile — 0.3

N

**FRANCIS MARION
NATIONAL FOREST**

Lofton Road

17

P 20

Forest
Service
houses

Dam

Dam

Impoundment

Tibwin Creek

Wildlife
opening

Viewing
Blind

Seasonally closed trail

Intracoastal Waterway

0.6 Curve near Tibwin Creek then cross the dam over an impoundment. You are looking out on tidal brackish marsh to your left and freshwater pond to your right. Ahead, turn along the impoundment.

0.9 Turn left, away from the impoundment, southbound.

1.1 Stay right as a dead-end trail goes left. Ahead, pass wild views to the southeast.

1.4 Keep straight as a seasonally closed trail leaves right. Open onto a dike with wide open marsh vistas.

1.6 The dike turns right. Look for the Intracoastal Waterway and Cape Romain in the distance. Wilderness views abound.

2.7 Turn right, northeasterly, as the trail you have been on heads north toward US 17.

3.1 Turn left at a four-way intersection, crossing a dam separating two impoundments. Keep north.

3.3 Return to the Forest Service houses, completing the loop. Backtrack north on gated FR 245.

3.5 Return to the trailhead, completing the hike.

Hiking with Children

Walking outdoors with little ones is all about seeing and experiencing nature through their eyes. Kids like to explore and have fun. They like to stop and point out bugs and plants, look under rocks, jump in puddles, and throw sticks. If you're taking a toddler or young child on a hike, start with a trail that you're familiar with. Trails that have interesting things for kids, like piles of leaves to play in or a small stream to wade through during the summer, will make the hike much more enjoyable for them and will keep them from getting bored.

You can keep your child's attention if you have a strategy before starting on the trail. Using games is not only an effective way to keep a child's attention, it's also a great way to teach him or her about nature. Quiz children on the names of plants and animals. If your children are old enough, let them carry their own daypacks filled with treats and a favorite (small) toy. So that you are sure to go at their pace and not yours, let them lead the way. Playing follow the leader works particularly well when you have a group of children. Have each child take a turn at being the leader. And head for home *before* the kids get tired or cranky so they'll want to hike again soon.

About the Author

Johnny Molloy is a writer and adventurer who has penned over fifty outdoor hiking, camping, and paddling guides, as well as true outdoor-adventure stories. His nonfiction passion started after reading *In Cold Blood* by Truman Capote, which his father had left lying around. After that, he delved into all manner of nonfiction reading, from *Strange But True Football Stories* to books about the Mississippi River, Lewis and Clark, and the Civil War. He has since focused his reading on early American history and Christian studies.

His outdoor passion started on a backpacking trip in Great Smoky Mountains National Park while attending the University of Tennessee. That first foray unleashed a love of the outdoors that has led Molloy to spend most of his time hiking, backpacking, canoe camping, and tent camping for the past three decades. Friends enjoyed his outdoor adventure stories, and one even suggested he write a book. He pursued his friend's idea and soon parlayed his love of the outdoors into an occupation.

Molloy writes for various magazines, websites, and newspapers. He continues writing and traveling extensively throughout the United States, engaging in a variety of outdoor pursuits. His non-outdoor interests include serving God as a Gideon and University of Tennessee sports. For the latest on Johnny, visit johnnymolloy.com.

Other Books by Johnny Molloy

50 Hikes in Alabama
50 Hikes in the Ozarks
50 Hikes in the North Georgia Mountains
50 Hikes in South Carolina
50 Hikes on Tennessee's Cumberland Plateau
60 Hikes within 60 Miles: San Antonio & Austin (with Tom Taylor)
60 Hikes within 60 Miles: Nashville
A Canoeing & Kayaking Guide to the Streams of Florida
A Canoeing & Kayaking Guide to the Streams of Kentucky (with Bob Sehlinger)
A Paddler's Guide to Everglades National Park
Backcountry Fishing: A Guide for Hikers, Backpackers and Paddlers
Beach & Coastal Camping in Florida
Beach & Coastal Camping in the Southeast
Best Easy Day Hikes: Chapel Hill, North Carolina
Best Easy Day Hikes: Charleston, South Carolina
Best Easy Day Hikes: Cincinnati
Best East Day Hikes: Greensboro/Winston-Salem
Best Easy Day Hikes: Jacksonville
Best Easy Day Hikes: Madison, Wisconsin
Best Easy Day Hikes: New River Gorge
Best Easy Day Hikes: Richmond
Best Easy Day Hikes: Tallahassee
Best Easy Day Hikes: Tampa Bay
Best Hikes Near Cincinnati
Best Hikes Near Columbus
Best Hikes Near: Raleigh, Durham and Chapel Hill
Best Hikes on the Appalachian Trail: South
The Best in Tent Camping: The Carolinas

The Best in Tent Camping: Colorado
The Best in Tent Camping: Georgia
The Best in Tent Camping: Kentucky
The Best in Tent Camping: Southern Appalachian & Smoky Mountains
The Best in Tent Camping: Tennessee
The Best in Tent Camping: West Virginia
The Best in Tent Camping: Wisconsin
Can't Miss Hikes in North Carolina's National Forests
Day & Overnight Hikes on Kentucky's Sheltowee Trace
Day & Overnight Hikes in West Virginia's Monongahela National Forest
Day Hiking Southwest Florida
Five Star Hikes: Chattanooga
Five Star Hikes: Knoxville
Five Star Hikes: Roanoke and the New River Valley
Five Star Hikes: Tri-Cities Tennessee and Virginia
From the Swamp to the Keys: A Paddle through Florida History
Hiking the Florida Trail: 1,100 Miles, 78 Days and Two Pairs of Boots
Hiking Mississippi
Hiking Through History: New England
Hiking Through History: Virginia
Hiking Waterfalls in Tennessee
Mount Rogers National Recreation Area Guidebook
The Hiking Trails of Florida's National Forests, Parks, and Preserves
Land Between the Lakes Outdoor Recreation Handbook
Long Trails of the Southeast
Outward Bound Canoeing Handbook
Paddling Georgia
Paddling Tennessee

Top Trails: Great Smoky Mountains National Park
Top Trails: Shenandoah National Park
Trial By Trail: Backpacking in the Smoky Mountains
Waterfalls of the Blue Ridge

AMERICAN HIKING SOCIETY

Because you
hike.
We're with you
every step of the way

American Hiking Society gives voice to the more than 75 million Americans who hike and is the only national organization that promotes and protects foot trails, the natural areas that surround them, and the hiking experience. Our work is inspiring and challenging, and is built on three pillars:

Volunteerism and Stewardship

We organize and coordinate nationally recognized programs—including Volunteer Vacations, National Trails Day ®, and the National Trails Fund— that help keep our trails open, safe, and enjoyable.

Policy and Advocacy

We work with Congress and federal agencies to ensure funding for trails, the preservation of natural areas, and the protection of the hiking experience.

Outreach and Education

We expand and support the national constituency of hikers through outreach and education as well as partnerships with other recreation and conservation organizations.

Join us in our efforts. Become an American Hiking Society member today!

American Hiking Society

1422 Fenwick Lane · Silver Spring, MD 20910 · (800) 972-8608
www.AmericanHiking.org · info@AmericanHiking.org